COUNTRY LIVING
AMERICAN
METALWARE

what is it? | what is it worth?

Joe L. Rosson
Helaine Fendelman

House of Collectibles

New York   Toronto   London   Sydney   Auckland

Important Notice: All the information, including valuations, in this book has been compiled from reliable sources, and efforts have been made to eliminate errors and questionable data. Nevertheless, the possibility of error, in a work of such immense scope, always exists. The publisher will not be responsible for any losses that may occur in the purchase, sale, or other transaction of items because of information contained herein. Readers who think they have discovered errors are invited to write and inform us, so they may be corrected in subsequent editions.

House of Collectibles and colophon are registered trademarks of Random House, Inc.

RANDOM HOUSE is a registered trademark of Random House, Inc.

Country Living is a trademark of Hearst Communications, Inc.

This book is available at special discounts for bulk purchases for sales promotions or premiums. Special editions, including personalized covers, excerpts of existing books, and corporate imprints, can be created in large quantities for special needs. For more information, write to Special Markets/Premium Sales, 1745 Broadway, MD 6-2, New York, NY 10019 or e-mail *specialmarkets@randomhouse.com.*

Please address inquiries about electronic licensing of any products for use on a network, in software, or on CD-ROM to the Subsidiary Rights Department, Random House Information Group, fax 212-572-6003.

Visit the House of Collectibles Web site: *www.houseofcollectibles.com*

Visit *Country Living* magazine: *www.countryliving.com*

Library of Congress Cataloging-in-Publication Data

Rosson, Joe.
    Country living American metalware : what is it? ; what is it worth? / Joe L. Rosson, Helaine Fendelman.
      p. cm.
    Includes bibliographical references and index.
    ISBN-13: 978-0-375-72118-2 (alk. paper)
     1. Metal-work—Collectors and collecting—United States.
 I. Fendelman, Helaine W. II. Title.

NK7804.R67 2007
739.0973'075—dc22   2006049770

Printed in China

10 9 8 7 6 5 4 3 2 1

ISBN: 978-0-375-72118-2

Acknowledgments

O nce again, we are very grateful to those who helped us write this book by supplying the necessary raw materials.

Our deepest gratitude goes to Dorothy Harris and the editors at Random House/House of Collectibles and Jacqueline Deval at Hearst Books, because without them, this project never would have left the launching pad. We also want to thank the art department at Random House for designing a book that is far more beautiful than we thought possible. We know it was extremely hard work, and we are knocked out by their efforts. We also acknowledge the immense contributions of Richard H. Crane, who kept us organized and did much of the hard work. He kept us going in difficult times and provided technical support that was indispensable.

We especially want to thank Skinner, Inc. of Boston and Bolton, Massachusetts, Northeast Auctions and Ronnie Bourgeault of Northeast Auctions of Portsmouth, New Hampshire, and Bertoia Auction Gallery of Vineland, New Jersey, for their generosity and help with both photographs and information. This book could not have been written without the support of these three fine institutions.

We also want to thank Jeffery Cupp, who made his collection available to us without complaining about the work and inconvenience we put him through. In addition our gratitude goes to Lauren Winer of Tiffany and Company, John Kuykendahl of the Glass Bazzaar in Knoxville, Tennessee, Dr. Bob Paddleford and his lovely wife, Chris, plus Roger Welsh, Elaine Tomber, and Betsey Creekmore.

Contents

PEWTER

COPPER, BRONZE, AND MIXED METALS

BRASS

COIN SILVER

STERLING SILVER

Introduction

A number of years ago in the dawn of our collecting, we wandered into a crowded antiques shop and were assaulted with a vast array of items that ranged from a forest of furniture to a giant earthenware teapot that was about the size of a Volkswagen—or at least it seemed that large, because it was suspended on a high shelf above our heads. It was a hot summer day in a sleepy southern town, and we had little to do but browse through this Aladdin's cave hoping to find the treasure of the ages.

In the bottom of a circa 1910 curved glass china cabinet there was a charming basket with elegant cutouts in the body and a bail-shaped handle also with cutouts along its length. It was metal with a heavy coat of dark oxidation, but it was charming, and underneath the tarnish, we detected the possibility of a gleam of silver. We carefully examined this piece, noted the mark on the bottom, which read "J. Ewan"—and nothing more.

On the side, there was a price tag for $29 and the dealer's opinion that this was a 19th-century basket. We hastily bought it, but could not resist asking the dealer what he thought it was. He replied that it was silver plated, and he knew that because solid silver pieces had either the word "sterling" or the number .925 on them. We thanked him for the basket and his input, and then, trying very hard to control the urgent need to get to a library, walked slowly and nonchalantly to our car—and sped away in a cloud of dust and anticipation.

Twenty minutes later, a quick perusal of a standard reference book on the subject of American silver told us that J. Ewan was the mark used by John Ewan, a Charleston, South Carolina, silversmith who had worked in coin silver from 1823 to 1852 in that fabled southern city. Coin silver, incidentally, is an American designation for a type of silver that is made from precious metal derived from melting down coins. It is generally between 89 and 90 percent pure silver, and was not made in this country (for the most part) after the end of the Civil War.

American coin silver is highly regarded by many collectors in the United States, and it is available in fairly large quantities in the form of various sizes of spoons. Coin silver hollowware items are often very hard to find and can be quite valuable. In addition, coin silver made in the South before the Civil War is quite rare, because much of it was destroyed during the conflict.

We were thrilled, because Charleston coin silver is so hard to find and a cake basket is a major piece, and at the time was valued at more than $4,000 for insurance replacement purposes. The gentleman who sold the basket to us made some assumptions that cost him a great deal of money, but he might not have made them if he had read this book.

This exploration of American-made metal wares begins with iron and proceeds to other metals, including tin, copper, bronze, pewter, silver (both coin and sterling silver), and silver plate (see the Glossary for definitions of these terms). Some of these pieces are very elegant, and some are the sort of thing that might be found in a cabinet or under a sink in any home in America.

Each piece has a description followed by a discussion of its origins and history plus some illuminating (we hope) side notes under the heading "What is it?" The next topic is "What is it worth?" and this needs a little explanation.

In some cases, we quote the "insurance replacement value," which should be defined as the amount of money it would take for a private individual to go out and replace an item if it were lost, stolen, or destroyed. In other words, the "insurance replacement value" is what it would take for an owner to find a comparable replacement item and purchase it from a retail source in an appropriate marketplace within a reasonable amount of time.

It is perhaps easiest to think of this as being a "retail" value, and this amount of money is not what a person can expect to receive for a similar object if he or she decided to sell. "Insurance replacement value" is the standard that is customarily used in the "What is it? What is it worth?" column that appears in *Country Living* magazine each month.

Those who are interested in selling items can expect to receive what is called "fair market value." This is defined by the Internal Revenue Service as "the price that property would sell for on the open market between a willing buyer and a willing seller, with neither being required to act, and both having reasonable knowledge of the relevant facts." Fair market value can be thought of as being "wholesale," and as a general rule, is 30 to 60 percent less than the "insurance replacement value."

In this book, we use the "insurance replacement value" standard unless it is otherwise clearly stated that the value was derived from an auction source and is the actual price paid at auction for the item under discussion. There was a time when auction prices were considered to be "fair market value," but that concept has changed over the past few decades.

The vast majority of all run-of-the-mill items that are sold at auctions still bring their "fair market value" when they are sold. In recent years, however, auctions across the nation have increasingly become outlets for very rare items that sell for sums that are closer to or even above what might have been considered to be "insurance replacement value" before the sale took place and the "astounding" price achieved. Therefore, prices realized at auction are open to interpretation as to which are "fair market value" and which are "retail" (or in some cases, above the retail level).

Whether an auction price fetched by a particular item is "fair market value" or retail depends on a number of factors, but the most important are the rarity, desirability, and condition of the item itself. After these considerations, items that bring prices significantly above "fair market value" might be the result of two or more bidders getting into an inexplicable "fight to the death," or in the case of an estate auction, two (or more) members of the family deciding that they must have a certain item no matter what the cost.

For the most part, in this book we quote auction prices of rare items that are, in our opinion, closer to "insurance replacement value" than they are to "fair market value."

IRON, STEEL, AND OTHER METALS

Item 1

"Highlander" Fireback

Valued at $3,500

Shaped slab of cast iron with embossed decorations of a figure in a crownlike hat holding a shield and a sword or long dagger. This figure is flanked by two flowering plants in pots and has the initials "A T," the words "New York," and the date "1767" above. The arch-shaped crest is surmounted with a pair of dolphins, and there are scrolling leaves and tendrils. The piece is 32 by 21 inches, and there is a crack at the center bottom.

What is it?

In the days before central heating and air-conditioning, the fireplace or the heating stove was a necessity if a family did not want to freeze during the harsh winters. Fireplaces that were set into outside walls were a real problem, because the intense heat caused the back walls to need frequent repairs.

To remedy this, foundries produced firebacks that protected the mortar and masonry and reflected heat into the room. An additional bonus to firebacks was that they were generally cast with decorative designs on their surfaces. These designs included scenes as well as images of animals, people, and/or geometrics. Sometimes, they included a foundry mark and a date of manufacture.

When the fireplace was lit, these raised designs provided an attractive pictorial element to the fire. When the fire was not lit, the

fireback provided sculptural and pictorial relief to what would otherwise have been just a cold, dark, uninteresting hole in the wall.

Firebacks were widely made in foundries in New England, and while firebacks were made in Pennsylvania, there were more heating stoves than firebacks manufactured there. This fireback was made in New York, but the initials "A T" that are found, along with the place of origin, have not been traced to a particular maker. Within the range of dated American firebacks, the 1767 date is neither early nor late, but its presence is a plus for collectors.

This design is called "The Highlander," and the figure is of a Scotsman.

What is it worth? This fireback sold at auction in August 2005 for $3,500.

Item 2
"Judith" Fireback

Valued at $600

Rectangular sheet of cast iron with an embossed image of two figures in a scene set in a tent. Both figures are women. One is holding a curved sword, and the other is holding a bag into which is being placed the head of a bearded man. In the lower quadrant there are swags, flowers, and a cornucopia with "Judith—XIII" in the center.

What is it?

This fireback is based on the Biblical story of Judith, which is included as a book in the Septuagint. This is a Greek translation of the Old Testament by Hellenistic Jews, which was written sometime between 250 BC and 100 BC. "Septuagint" means "70" and was supposedly done in 72 days by 72 scholars (thus the name), but it is not included in the Hebrew Bible and is placed in the Apocrypha of Christian Bibles.

Judith means "Jewess," and hers is the story of a widow who saved the city of Bethulia from destruction by Holofernes, the general sent by Nabuchodonosor, king of Nineveh, to vanquish the Jews. Other sources say the king was Nebuchadnezzar, king of Assyria, but this particular king is generally associated with Babylon. This fast and loose use of Nebuchadnezzar's name and place of kingship may indicate that the story of Judith is a folktale intended to convey a lesson rather than be the literal truth.

In any event, the city was besieged and suffering from famine. It was about to surrender when Judith volunteered to save the city from destruction. She entered Holofernes's camp and beguiled him with her beauty, and the general wished to seduce her. But as he lay drunk, Judith removed his sword from its scabbard as it hung on a pillar that was by Holofernes's bed. She then took the general by his hair and cut off his head with two strokes.

She rolled the body in the bed curtains and gave the head to her maid, who put it in her "wallet" or bag, and they left the city unchallenged. Upon returning to Bethulia, Judith triumphantly showed the head to the populace. The citizens were then inspired to attack the enemy's camp and were victorious.

The story of the beheading of Holofernes and placing the head in the "wallet" of the maid is told on this fireback, and it is noted below the scene that this part of the story can be found in Judith Chapter XIII (13). Imagine a family in the mid- to late 18th century sitting in front of the fireplace watching the flames flicker and having this scene from the story of Judith illuminated before them. It provided a chance to teach the children that belief in God can bring victory even to the weakest.

In this case, the fireback not only protected the fireplace brick from damage but also provided a powerful instructional tool that could be used on those long winter nights.

What is it worth?

This undated fireback with its religious theme sold at auction in August 2005 for $600.

Item
Wafer Iron

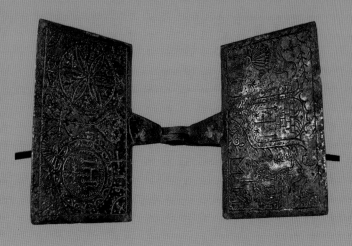

What is it? Modern Americans are familiar with waffle irons into which batter is poured and after baking, a crisp, golden brown confection with indentations all over its surface emerges to be slathered with butter and either syrup or powdered sugar (or both).

Waffle irons are basically from the 19th century and later, but as early as the 14th century people were using a special apparatus to make a similar product made from sugar and eggs called a wafer. Wafer irons came in a great variety of designs. Some had square paddles, others had paddles that were rectangular, circular, or oval. Most of them had some sort of grid on the inside surface to hold the batter in place and to leave a pattern on the surface of the finished wafer.

Some of these patterns were quite simple and included flowers, geometrics, signatures, religious symbols, and occasionally, a date. Originally, these thin, crisp wafers were made to be used on religious holidays, but later they were used widely for other special occasions. The cross and other religious symbols seen on the inside surface of this piece suggest that it might have been crafted with the idea of making wafers to celebrate a religious event, or it may just have been made for a devout family.

Valued at $2,500

Iron utensil with an overall length of 36 1/2 inches. The 8 3/4 by 5 1/4-inch paddles at the end of the long handles have embossed designs on either side. One side has two circles, one with a typical starflower and a fan above and "H" with a cross above, plus hearts. The other side has two birds flanking a crest. The piece is dated 1779.

The long handles allowed the user to stand back from the fire as the wafer was being baked so that he or she would not be scorched by the intense heat. It is probable that many, if not most, wafer irons found in this country were made in England and exported to America, but the piece pictured here has all the signs of having been made on these shores.

It was completely handmade by a blacksmith. The designs are incised in a somewhat crude manner, which might be more explicable when it is understood that all the images had to be cut into the iron in mirror image so that when the wafer was finished, all the symbols would be readable to the person who was about to enjoy this sweet treat.

Some of the symbols on this wafer iron indicate that it may have been made in one of the Moravian communities in Pennsylvania, and the date is either the actual date of manufacture or a date to commemorate some sort of special event.

What is it worth? This late-18th-century wafer iron has an insurance replacement value of $2,500.

Item 4

Iron and Brass Candlestand

Valued at $8,000

Iron and brass adjustable candlestand that is 60 3/4 inches tall. It has an arched tripod base and a long spike in the center topped with a small finial and a small circular knop on the shaft about two-thirds of the way down. The iron central post supports a bar with two candle cups that have brass bobeches below. These are above a simple rectangular sliding arm with two scrolled hooks.

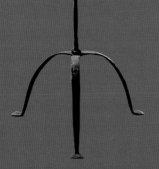

What is it?

Candlestands such as this one are one of the most sought-after forms of lighting used in America. They are, however, widely faked and reproduced, and great care should be taken in evaluating this type of lighting device before purchase.

Most of these candlestands are between 5 and 6 feet tall, with some being just a bit taller and others a bit shorter—but seldom less than about 50 inches. They usually have arched tripod bases, but bases with straight tripod legs are known. The legs are generally plain and terminate in pads called "penny feet," but twisted metal legs were sometimes used, as were other kinds of feet.

Most of these candlestands are iron, and they may or may not have brass accents. When they are found with this additional metal, the brass is usually used to make the finial, the candle cups, and/or ring decoration (or decorations) on the shafts above the feet. The use of brass made these candlestands more pleasing to the eye, but they increased the amount of work necessary to maintain them because the brass had to be polished regularly, whereas the iron only needed to be protected from rust.

The small iron finial on the piece pictured to the left is simply an elongated ball-shaped extension of the pole. Sometimes the finials were much fancier and might be composed of scrolling curls of metal or be in the shape of a flame or urn.

These candlestands often offered the home owner options for the type of lighting that was going to be used in the home. Candles, for example, were expensive, and they may have been used in these stands only for special occasions. The hooks on this example may be there to hold "Betty," or grease lamps, which were far more economical to operate because they used oil or grease rather than expensive candles.

Some candlestands had rush holders, pincerlike devices generally next to the candle cup that were intended to secure a rush head (a rush is a grasslike marsh plant in the family Juncaceae). These heads were dipped in tallow, and when they were lighted, they gave off a very weak light that was smoky and odiferous.

Candlestands similar to this one were made in both America and England. This one is blacksmith made, thought to be American, and all original.

What is it worth?

This particular candlestand sold at auction in August 2005 for $8,000.

Item 5
Griswold Skillet

Valued at $25

Cast-iron skillet, 14 inches long from handle to far rim with a diameter of 9 3/4 inches from pouring spout to pouring spout. On the bottom, the piece is marked "Cast Iron Skillet," "6," "Erie, Pa. U.S.A.," and "699," with a cross within two concentric circles and "Griswold" written in block letters.

What is it? The Selden & Griswold Company was founded in Erie, Pennsylvania, in 1865 by Samuel and John Card Selden and Matthew Griswold. Matthew Griswold, John Card Selden's brother-in-law, was a member of a distinguished Connecticut family and was born in 1833 in Old Lyme. He was a farmer there until he moved to Erie and went into partnership with the Selden brothers.

The foundry, on the Erie Extension Canal, was a successor to a maker of hardware called the Butt Factory, which took its name from the butt hinges it manufactured. Selden and Griswold expanded over the years. In 1884, Matthew Griswold bought out the Selden interest and the firm became the Griswold Manufacturing Company, which was formally chartered in 1897.

Griswold is often said to have made the finest cast-iron ware in the United States, but they also have the distinction of being credited with making the first pieces of aluminum cookware. Aluminum is one of the most abundant elements in the earth's crust, but before 1886 there was no practical or economical way to extract it from its ore, bauxite.

Before Charles Martin Hall and Paul Heroult discovered how to use electricity to extract the metal in 1886, aluminum was such a precious metal that it was sometimes used to make jewelry. Around 1890, Arthur Vining Davis came to Griswold with the idea of making cast aluminum cookware.

According to legend, Griswold asked his secretary what was the one piece of kitchen equipment that a woman would like to have made from a material that was lighter than cast iron. She replied, a teakettle, and Griswold had a mold made and taken to the Pittsburgh Reduction Company to be cast in the new metal. The Pittsburgh Reduction Company later became known as the Aluminum Corporation of America or Alcoa (ALCOA), and Arthur Vining Davis was its president and later chairman of the board.

One of the marks used by the Griswold Manufacturing Company and the one found on the skillet discussed here.

American Metalware   11

Over the years, Griswold made an astonishing variety of cast-iron products. Modern collectors are familiar with the skillets, Dutch ovens, corn-stick pans, waffle irons, and muffin pans, but Griswold made much more. These items include such things as umbrella stands, mailboxes, gas ranges, cuspidors (especially a model on wheels), tobacco cutters, cake molds, mortars and pestles, sundials, and fruit and lard presses.

Griswold products can be found marked in a variety of ways. The earliest mark was just the word "Erie," but a more elaborate early logo consisted of the image of a spider in a web with the word "Erie" on its back (a "spider," incidentally, is the name given to a cast-iron frying pan with a rounded bottom and short legs). Another mark is a diamond-shaped device with the name Griswold's at the top, "Erie" in the middle, and "Extra Finished Ware" below.

The most commonly seen trademarks, however, are the ones with a cross inside a double circle with the name Griswold inscribed across the crosspiece written in either block or slanted letters. The ones with the slanted Griswold are a little earlier and preferred by collectors, but they are not as commonly found as the block letter logos.

The block letter insignias can be found in two sizes: a large example that can nearly cover the bottom of a frying pan, and a small one that occupies the middle area. The skillet pictured here has the large logo. It is a size 6 and pattern number 699. This model is flat bottomed and has no heat ring around the bottom. The pattern number for the size 6 with the heat ring is 699B.

Griswold cast iron came in a variety of finishes. The Extra Finish Ware, for which the company is noted, has a polished interior, and in some cases even the top of the handle has been polished. Another was called Plain Iron, and these Griswold items were completely unpolished. Collectors like the Extra Finish Ware, but this particular skillet has the Plain Iron surface.

All the Griswolds had left the company by 1947, but it continued for a while before closing on December 7, 1957. Reportedly, the Griswold name was used later by other companies, and although these pieces are collectible, they are not as eagerly sought as items from the pre-1958 production are.

What is it worth?
Griswold skillets with a heat ring are generally more valuable than ones without. The number 6 size is fairly easy to find and has an insurance replacement value of $25. With the heat ring, that price almost doubles.

Related item

Shallow dish, rectangular with canted corners. The piece is 11 1/2 inches long from tab handle to tab handle and 6 inches wide. The outside surface is a Chinese red, and the interior is ivory. The bottom is marked "Griswold" in the crossbar of a cross that is inside two concentric rings. The number "81" is on the bottom as well. The piece shows much wear, with some discoloration.

What is it?

There is no question that this piece was loved and used extensively. The owner remembers her mother baking casseroles in this dish, and the interior shows shadowy signs of past dinners that could not be completely removed no matter how much "elbow grease" and cleaning products were applied.

When it was given to us for inclusion in this book, the owner—who is a very dear friend and producer of our television show—made it clear that this piece was precious, that it was "very old," and most important, that it was not something she had collected, but was her mother's, and there were fond memories attached. This is very important, because nostalgia is one of the main reasons for collecting kitchenware. Many people cannot resist an old mixing bowl or a battered cast-iron skillet because it reminds them of the meals their mothers and grandmothers made in the distant past when life was simpler and safer.

Griswold started putting colorful porcelain finishes on cast iron in the late 1920s. One of the company's advertisements touts this dish and others like it as "New Joy for Your Kitchen!" Initially, pieces were manufactured in shades of Mandarin Red, Canary Yellow, Jade Green, and Turquoise Blue. The enamel colors were found on the outside of these pieces, while the interiors were plain.

This early Griswold porcelain finish can be found on skillets, skillet covers, and Dutch ovens, and this surface was said to "clean like china." A little later in the 1940s and '50s Griswold made a line of cast iron with bi-colored finishes. These pieces included skillets, skillet covers, corn-stick pans, various sizes of casserole dishes (both covered and uncovered), Dutch ovens, and an oval roaster.

What is it worth?

In perfect or near perfect condition, the insurance replacement value of this #81 casserole dish is $85. With the staining and chipping, the value of this piece is closer to $50.

Item 6
Golfer Doorstop

Valued at $500

Figure of a man in a snap-brim hat holding a golf club preparing to putt. The golfer is wearing a belted jacket and knickers, and the piece is 8 3/8 inches tall by 7 inches wide. The piece is made of iron and painted primarily in shades of brown and green.

There is some loss to the paint, and the piece is unsigned.

What is it? In the days before central heating and air-conditioning, good ventilation was necessary to keep homes as cool as possible during hot weather, and doorstops were necessary pieces of household equipment. These devices were also used to keep doors closed during cold weather when chilly winds might blow a door open and dissipate all the precious warmth.

These items are thought to have originated in England, where they are called doorporters, and from the late 19th century through the present day, they have been made in a vast variety of forms. Some of the most popular doorstops are in the shapes of various kinds of dogs, and collectors find doorstops that look like Boston terriers, English bulldogs, Saint Bernards, German shepherds, Scotties, beagles, dachshunds, basset hounds, Prince Charles spaniels, Irish setters, and even Russian wolfhounds.

Images of cats, monkeys, birds, people, camels, squirrels, owls, horses, elephants, fish, cows, frogs, turtles, alligators, baskets of flowers, houses, castles, lighthouses, windmills, ships, stagecoaches, lanterns, gnomes, and many others can be found as well. There are at least two well-known representations of men playing golf. One shows the golfer with the club over his shoulder about to swing and drive the ball down the fairway, and the other is the piece pictured here.

Of these two, the one with the golfer about to drive the ball is the rarer. However, there is another golf-related doorstop that is even more valuable. That is one in the shape of the caddy struggling with a golf bag that appears to be almost as large as he is. This piece came in two different paint treatments: one showed the caddy as an African-American, and the other as a Caucasian.

Both the golfer swinging and the golfer putting are thought to have been made by the Hubley Manufacturing Company of Lancaster, Pennsylvania. The name Hubley is an important one in the toy industry. They began manufacturing cast-iron toys around 1894 and made such items as toy coal stoves, circus wagons, and mechanical banks as well as cast-iron vehicles.

In the 1920s Hubley expanded their Metal Art Goods line and began making items that might best be described as giftware and household items. These included ashtrays, bookends, doorstops, and novelty wares. At one time, Hubley was the world's largest producer of cast-iron toys and cap pistols. Unfortunately, by the 1940s cast-iron toys were out of fashion, and because of their weight, the cost of distributing them had become prohibitive and the company began making die-cast zinc alloy toys.

During World War II, Hubley largely switched to war production and made bomb fuses. Hubley was bought by Gabriel Industries in 1965 and still makes such things as cap pistols and toy vehicles.

The putting golfer pictured here is circa 1930 and has most of its original paint. Original paint is very important to collectors of vintage doorstops, and pieces that have been repainted often go begging. Caution is advised when purchasing doorstops because there are many reproductions on the market; the buyer should beware.

What is it worth? In this condition, the putting golfer is worth $500.

Item 7
House Doorstop

Valued at $192.50

Cast-iron doorstop in the form of a
Cape Cod–style house complete with
lawn, garden, and sidewalk. It is 8 1/2
inches long and has its original paint
in pristine condition.

What is it? Some of the more commonly found types of doorstops are in the shape of houses and cottages. These came in a vast array of shapes and styles that ranged from "Ann Hathaway's Cottage" to a castle on top of a hill. There were houses with peaked roofs, houses smothered in flowers, houses with two stories, and the ubiquitous Cape Cod–style cottage.

The one shown on the previous page was made by the Albany Foundry Company, which was in operation on VanRensselaer Island just south of Albany, New York. They were in business from 1897 to 1932, but when this area was incorporated into the Port of Albany, the foundry closed.

The Albany Foundry Company made a variety of cast-iron items such as bookends, andirons, hitching posts, and doorstops, which they customarily sold undecorated with only a gray iron finish. Customers, however, could order their doorstops and other items painted, and the company would accommodate their request.

The company price list for 1924 reveals that the doorstops were sold relatively cheaply, with prices ranging from 50 cents to $2 each. In addition, the Albany Foundry Company offered to drill and tap some of their doorstops (for a nominal charge) so they could be used as electric lamp bases.

The 1924 catalog shows a wide variety of doorstops, including one in the form of a ship with billowing sails, a cockatoo, a stag, a rabbit in a top hat, a child, and several baskets of flowers in various designs. They did offer a Cape Cod–style house very similar to the one pictured above, but about a half an inch longer.

The beautiful condition of the paint on this circa 1920 Albany Foundry Company doorstop makes it a desirable find for collectors.

What is it worth? This doorstop sold at auction in May 2005 for $192.50.

Item 8
Squirrel Mill Weight

$2,500
Figure of a squirrel with curled tail standing on a rectangular plinth.
It is 17 1/2 inches tall and 14 inches at its widest. It is cast iron and has a pierced eye, with holes in the paw and at the base. Its silvered surface shows rust spots and a great deal of wear.

What is it?

It is a bit hard to imagine the intended purpose for a heavy piece of iron such as this one. It is too tall to be a doorstop, and the hole configuration on the body suggests that it might have had a more mechanical function.

This is actually a mill weight that was part of a windmill used to pump water (and in some rare cases grind grain) on farms around the world and across the United States. Typically, wind rotates the blades of the windmill, which, in turn, operates a pump that draws water from a well and dumps it into an aboveground reservoir for use by both man and beast.

Windmills usually consisted of an arrangement of fanlike blades set atop a high trestle tower, and weights were used to act as a counterbalance for the rotating blades. Mill weights customarily weighed between 8 and 85 pounds and can be found in a wide variety of shapes such as cows, horses, chickens, eagles, buffalos, and squirrels as well as geometric designs and letters of the alphabet.

Sometimes, they can be found stamped with the name of their manufacturer, and examples with their original paint or with a rusty patina are particularly desirable. It is said that at one time there were more than 1,500 manufacturers of windmills in the United States. Some of these are the Fairbury Windmill Company of Fairbury, Nebraska, the Nebraska Elgin Wind Power and Pump Company of Elgin, Illinois, and the Dempster Manufacturing Company of Des Moines, Iowa.

Mill weights are often associated with midwestern farms because the winds rushing across the plains made these devices very practical for that region, but they also were used on farms in the south and in the east as well as in cities as big as New York. There is some difference of opinion about who invented the American windmill. One source says Daniel Halladay, a New England mechanic, made the first commercially successful windmill in 1854. However, another source credits John Burnham for having constructed and tested a windmill in Ellington, Connecticut, also in 1854.

Collectors need to be aware that reproductions abound, and a simple perusal of the Internet will reveal a number of new mill weights being offered for sale.

What is it worth?

This squirrel mill weight sold at auction in August 2005 for $2,500.

Related items

1 Figure of a bull with the word "BOSS" written across its body in bold block letters on both sides. It has a base that makes it appear as if the bovine is striding across rocky ground. The figure is anatomically correct and made from cast iron. It was made in two pieces that were joined together with a bolt and is 12 1/2 inches high by 14 1/4 inches long.

What is it?
It is possible to look at this mill weight and think that BOSS is short for Bossie, a common nickname for animals of the bovine persuasion, or that maybe the bull itself was named BOSS. Neither, however, is the case.

This weight was used on the Boss Vaneless Windmill, which was manufactured by the Dempster Manufacturing Company of Des Moines, Iowa. This company was founded in 1878 and is still in business. This particular "BOSS" bull weight was made circa 1900.

What is it worth?
This weight sold at auction in August 2005 for $1,600. Replicas of it are available on the Internet. The rusty patina on this example is comforting, but unscrupulous sellers often bury iron weights for months or treat them artificially to try to arrive at a similar finish.

2 Iron figure of a rooster mounted to an associated (not original) plinth. The tail is grooved and shaped like a rainbow, and the body is painted with original white, red, and yellow paint. The piece, made from cast iron, is 21 1/2 inches tall and 16 inches wide.

What is it?
Mill weights such as this one have a wonderful sculptural quality that attracts collectors of country Americana. Such pieces may have started out as utilitarian objects, but now they are seen as highly decorative and are considered by many to have attained a status of folk art.

Originality of surface is very important to this kind of object. This means original paint in excellent condition or an honest rusty surface showing that the object hung out in every type of weather for a number of years is optimum to peak collector interest. Mill weights in the shape of roosters are commonly found, but the piece pictured here has a very nice form, and the condition of its original paint is superior.

What is it worth?
In August 2005, this rooster sold for $1,750.

Item 9
"Possum and Taters" Still Bank

What is it? In the early 20th century, political cartoons were a powerful source of American iconography. Theodore Roosevelt, for example, was depicted in a 1902 *Washington Star* newspaper refusing to shoot a bear cub while on a hunting trip in Mississippi. This image soon became enshrined as "Teddy's bear," which soon led to the lovable stuffed toy known as the Teddy Bear.

Before his term ended in 1909, Roosevelt chose William Howard Taft as his successor. In a political postcard of the day, Roosevelt was depicted as a "Teddy Bear" shaking hands with fat old "Billy Possum" on the way to the White House. That same year, J. M. Harper of Chicago, Illinois, designed and copyrighted a bank that illustrated the Billy Possum part of this scene with the intention of poking some fun at the corpulent Taft, who had indeed been elected president.

Another maker of banks and toys, the Arcade Manufacturing Company of Freeport, Illinois, is thought to have made a "still" bank that held President Taft up to derision as well. Called the "Eggman" or "Taft" bank, this circa 1910 bank shows a figure re-

Valued at $8,800

Bank in the form of an opossum with a scattering of objects underneath that are said to be potatoes. Embossed on the base is "Possum and Taters" on one side and "Billy Possum" on the other. The opossum figure has a coin slot at the top of its back, and the piece is 4 3/4 inches long by 3 inches tall. It is made from iron and painted gray with a gold-and-black base. There is expected wear to the paint. This piece is signed on the bottom edge, "J. M. Harper Copyright 1909."

sembling Taft shaped like an egg with a top hat on and a watch fob hanging from his vest pocket.

Between 1902 and 1909, Harper patented fifteen "still" (meaning they had no moving parts) penny banks. He seemed to specialize in American presidents and made busts of such figures as Abraham Lincoln, George Washington, Ulysses S. Grant, William McKinley, Grover Cleveland, and Theodore Roosevelt.

All the busts rest on an old-fashioned safe, and the one of President McKinley recently brought more than $5,000 at auction. The Lincoln brought slightly less at around $3,500, and the Washington sold for the least of all at a bit less than $2,000.

Harper did not cast these himself but had them made at the Chicago Hardware Foundry Company in North Chicago, which had been established in 1897 to produce gray iron castings. Harper's tribute to William Howard Taft was cast in two pieces and is held together by a single flat-head screw. It is considered to be quite rare by collectors.

What is it worth? This bank sold at auction in May 2005 for $8,800.

Still bank, iron with bronze- or copper-colored finish. The piece has the image of three Native Americans, a warrior, a woman, and a small child. It is 5 inches wide and 3 7/8 inches high. There is a coin slot behind the warrior's headdress.

What is it?

Like the "still" bank "Possum and Taters" discussed previously, this example was designed by J. M. Harper and cast by the Chicago Hardware Foundry Company. It was copyrighted in 1905 and depicts a Native American family; collectors generally call it the Indian Family Bank.

This bank was made at a time when political correctness was not an issue, and the three individuals shown are usually identified as Plains Indians, probably Sioux. The man is usually described as a "warrior" dressed in his feathered war bonnet and bear claw necklace. He is flanked by his "squaw" and their "papoose."

The Harper Indian Family Bank was made in two sections held together with a flat-head screw. This piece is in excellent condition with its original surface. It is considered a hard-to-find "still" bank.

What is it worth?

This bank sold at auction in May 2005 for $1,760.

Item 10
Bank Building Mechanical Bank

Valued at $1,800

Cast-iron model of a building with a front door with fan light above that opens to reveal the figure of a man. The roof has two chimneys and two dormer windows on each side of the slanting roof. On the lower story, there are two windows on each side except the front. On the side is impressed "Pat'd June 25 1872 Oct 23 1873." The piece is 6 3/4 inches tall and 4 1/2 inches wide.

What is it?

Thrift was a lesson that most Victorian parents wanted to teach their children, and to do this they often gave them a bank in which to save their pennies. Before the late 1860s, banks were "still." In other words, they did not do anything but receive and house coins when they were put in a slot.

These early still banks were often shaped like safes, jugs, even animals. Then, in 1869, John Hall of Watertown, Massachusetts, was granted a patent for a bank that moved. In Hall's original design a lever was pushed, a cupola on top of the "Hall's Excelsior Bank" opened, and a teller sitting in front of a desk popped up. When these were manufactured by the J. & E. Stevens Company, a wooden figure of a monkey was substituted for the human bank teller. In this post–Civil War era when store-bought toys were relatively rare, children must have thought this was very amusing—if not rather amazing.

When a coin was placed on the monkey's desk, the weight caused the money to descend and be deposited in the bank. Unfortunately, to retrieve the savings, the bank had to be disassembled. This difficult task required tools, and successful reassembly was not a sure or easy thing.

The bank pictured on the preceding page is similar to this in that it is a bank building. When the front door is opened, a human teller with a tray is revealed. When the money is placed on the teller's tray and the door is closed, the money is deposited in a slot in the teller's cage.

Like the Hall's Excelsior Bank, this bank is attributed to the J. & E. Stevens Company, which was established in 1843 by brothers John and Elisha Stevens. They built their plant in "Frog Hollow Valley," next to the Connecticut River in Cromwell, Connecticut.

The company's first production was hardware and tools, but they soon branched out to making toys and cap pistols. In 1890, J. & E. Stevens abandoned the production of hardware and tools and began to concentrate on toys and banks, both still and mechanical. The company continued making banks until 1928, when they discontinued them in favor of making cap pistols. They closed at the beginning of World War II because of the shortage of iron for nonmilitary purposes.

This example is in relatively good condition, but it does have a broken spring and there is damage to the paint.

What is it worth?

In this condition with a broken spring and worn paint, the value is $1,800.

Item 11
"Tammany" Mechanical
Bank

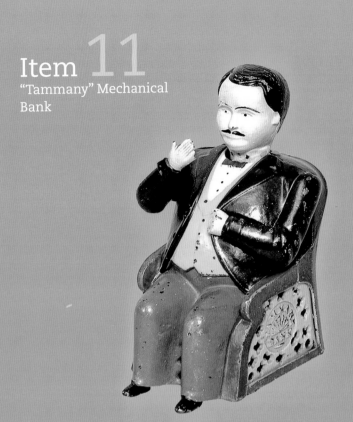

$1,320
Mechanical bank in the form of a man
sitting in a chair with a raised right arm.
On the openwork side is a circle with a
raised fan in the center surrounded by
the words "Tammany Bank." The figure is
painted iron and wears a brown coat
over a yellow vest and brown trousers. It
is 6 inches tall, 4 1/2 inches long, and 3
1/2 inches wide. The paint is original and
in pristine condition.

What is it? Some people call this the "Little Fat Man" mechanical bank, but it is really meant to suggest an effigy of William Marcy Tweed—better known to the world as "Boss Tweed." From the 1850s to the early 1870s, Tweed was associated with Tammany Hall, a name commonly given to the New York City Democratic political machine as well as the location that was their headquarters.

After the end of the American Revolutionary War, a number of societies sprang up to promote various political and economic causes. One of these was the Tammany Society, which was named after Chief Tamanend, who signed a treaty with William Penn. Tammany had branches in several cities, but the one that we now know and remember is the one in New York City.

It was founded in 1786 and was also known as the Columbian Order of New York City. At one point this Tammany Society was under the control of Aaron Burr, and the group also helped elect Andrew Jackson in both 1828 and 1832. Tammany gained a lot of its influence by helping immigrants find jobs and get settled in their new environment, and then helped them become naturalized United States citizens quickly. The immigrants were grateful for this assistance and were very loyal to the way that Tammany Hall wanted them to vote.

William Marcy Tweed (1823–78) was a chair maker by trade, but he was also a volunteer fireman. He used this to advance himself politically, and in 1851 he was elected a New York City alderman. Through elections and the appointment of friends, he established what became known as the "Tweed Ring," and in the 1860s and early 1870s they are said to have controlled all the Democratic Party's nominations in New York City and to a lesser extent in New York State.

By 1868, Tweed was the "boss" of New York's Tammany Hall organization. It is said that Tweed engineered the New York City charter that was enacted in 1870, a document that put the city in the hands of people whom Tweed controlled. Over a two-year period, it is said that the "Tweed Ring" stole more than $200,000,000 from the City of New York and its taxpayers. How did they do it? One way was to overcharge the city for services and goods.

For example, they charged the city $13,000,000 to build a new court house that cost only $250,000 to construct, and $3,000,000 for two years worth of stationery and printing. The overages were distributed between Tweed and his cronies. But this arrangement led to Tweed's downfall when a disgruntled member of the ring blew the whistle in 1871 because he believed he was being cheated out of a fair share of the spoils. He talked to the newspapers, which subsequently led to the election of opposition candidates in 1871. Tweed was convicted for his crimes in 1873 and sentenced to twelve years in jail—but served only one. He then went to debtors' prison but fled to Cuba at his first opportunity. Hounded by authorities, Tweed relocated to Spain, where he was recaptured and returned to the United States in 1876. He died in prison just two years later.

On December 23, 1873, John Hall patented a mechanical "Tammany Hall" bank with the likeness of a man who is supposed to suggest "Boss" Tweed. An example of this rather commonly found mechanical bank is shown here.

When a coin is placed in the figure's raised hand, the appendage quickly drops the money into his pocket with a brief bow of the head. This is supposed to depict a politician taking graft for purposes of preferment.

This is another bank manufactured by the J. & E. Stevens Company of Cromwell, Connecticut, which was established in 1843 by brothers John and Elisha Stevens. The factory was in a valley called Frog Hollow, which got its name because of all the croaking amphibians that inhabited the stream and pond that provided power to the plant.

The "Tammany Bank" is found in several versions. In some there is no lettering in the circle on the chair, and colors of the seated figure's coat can vary. This particular example is in almost pristine condition.

What is it worth? In May 2005, this bank sold at auction for $1,320.

Item 12
"Uncle Sam" Mechanical Bank

Valued at $6,050

Mechanical bank in the shape of Uncle Sam standing on a platform with a raised eagle and a banner that reads "Uncle Sam" on the front and the word "Bank" on the side. A satchel at the feet of the figure is embossed "U. S." The lower jaw of the figure is on pivots and moves easily up and down, and the satchel opens when a button is pressed on the base. The piece is 11 1/2 inches tall and the base is 5 inches wide on each side. The base plate has been repaired and repainted, but the paint on the rest of the piece is in good to excellent condition with original pink face, green umbrella, and red-and-white-striped pants.

What is it?

Uncle Sam has a long history in American folklore, but his actual origins are a bit hazy. Many think he is based on the real-life Samuel Wilson, who was born in Arlington, Massachusetts, in 1766.

During the War of 1812, Wilson provided meat to the U.S. Army, and the barrels in which he customarily shipped his product were all marked "U. S." for "United States." A joke began to circulate that the initials actually stood for "Uncle Sam" Wilson, and by 1813 the name had appeared in newspapers; in 1816 it was used in a book. However, how the name "Uncle Sam" came to symbolize the American federal government is open to some speculation.

"Uncle Sam" may actually be an amalgamation of two other folkloric figures: Yankee Doodle and Brother Jonathan. Of these two, Yankee Doodle is probably the oldest, because it is the title of a song sung in derision by British military officers to mock the American troops during the French and Indian War.

The word "Yankee" is thought to have been derived from the Dutch nickname for Americans, which was "Jan Kees," or "John Cheese," and a "Doodle" is a simpleton or fool. When the tide of the Revolutionary War was turning in the favor of the Americans, the "Yankees" adopted the song as their own and threw it back in triumph at the British, and the personification of "Yankee Doodle" was adopted as a symbol of the new United States.

The character Brother Jonathan also started as a term of derision. This was the name American loyalists directed at American patriots during the Revolutionary War. At the time, he was depicted as a colonial man in a tricorn hat with a military coat, but there may have been a real Brother Jonathan, because it was what George Washington sometimes affectionately called Jonathan Turnbull (1710–85), who was governor of Connecticut.

Political cartoonist Thomas Nast is often credited with giving us the image of Uncle Sam that we know today. But when he was drawing, he also represented both Yankee Doodle and Brother Jonathan, and his rendition of this latter figure closely resembles Uncle Sam because both were shown wearing star-spangled red, white, and blue costumes.

Like Yankee Doodle, Nast usually drew Brother Jonathan with a feather in his cap, but of course, Uncle Sam was depicted with a top hat that did not have a feather. In addition, Brother Jonathan was beardless, whereas Uncle Sam had a distinctive goatee.

The mechanical bank pictured here was designed by Charles G. Shepard and Peter Adams and produced by the Shepard Hardware Company of Buffalo, New York. It was patented in 1886, and when a coin was placed in Uncle Sam's hand and a lever was pressed on the base, the satchel would open, the coin would drop in, and Uncle Sam's mouth would move up and down as if saying, "Thank you!"

Shepard Hardware was a large operation that specialized in making iron castings and a variety of hardware items, and in 1882 they began making mechanical banks, including one in the form of a "Punch and Judy" puppet show. In 1892, the mechanical bank line was sold to the J. & E. Stevens Company of Cromwell, Connecticut (actually located in the "Frog Hollow" Valley), which continued making the line until around the turn of the 20th century.

Shepard was a prolific maker of mechanical banks, and many of their designs were very colorful. Unfortunately, the company failed to put a primer coat under their elaborate paint schemes. As a result, many Shepard banks have lost their original paint and have either been repainted or gone to rust. The paint on the example shown here is in much better than average condition.

What is it worth? This bank sold at auction in May 2005 for $6,050.

Item 13

"Lighthouse" Semi-Mechanical Bank

Valued at $764

Cast-iron bank in the form of a lighthouse on a rocky shore with signal tower. The piece is painted red with a green painted base, and the paint is very worn. The hose-shaped structure has a slot in the roof and the lighthouse tower has evenly spaced windowlike holes up the side. The piece is 10 3/8 inches tall and 6 3/8 inches long.

What is it? This bank is, appropriately, known as "The Lighthouse Bank," and it was made circa 1890 by an unknown company. Some people call this a mechanical bank. Others, however, classify it as a "semi-mechanical" bank because its action is not as evident to the eye as it is on some of the true mechanical banks, which may shoot a penny into a slot in a castle wall or show Uncle Sam dropping a penny into a bag marked "U. S."

To operate this bank, a coin (some sources say the coin is supposed to be a penny, but a nickel is the correct denomination) is inserted into the slot at the top of the lighthouse tower. It is held there by two flat springs until the knob, which forms the top of the tower, is turned and the coin falls down the length of the shaft. Interestingly, the two springs that hold the coin until it is dropped also prevent the removal of the coin once it is inserted and dropped—so once the coin is in there, it is in there to stay.

When it was new, the windows were numbered up the side of the tower. One side had even numbers 10 to 90, and the other side had odd numbers 15 to 85. When coins 98 to 100 were inserted in the slot, the mechanism would allow the knob to be pressed down and the drawer in the coin receptacle would open, allowing the bank to be emptied. Coins of various denominations could be inserted into the house itself, and these could be removed easily by opening a round cover on the bottom of the bank.

Fresh from the factory, these numbers were printed in gold, which made them very striking against the red of the tower. The sliding drawer used to empty the tower is also red, but the knob on top of the lighthouse and the ring just under it were nickel plated. The rocky base was a japanned or varnished black, and the houselike structure was similarly adorned.

The piece pictured to the left has an old repaint in which the gold numbers are missing, and the base has been painted green, which actually shows the rocky nature in more detail than the original color scheme did.

What is it worth? This piece sold at auction in February 2005 for $764. This price is rather low because of the repaint. Collectors of toys and banks generally disdain repaints, and if this piece were in perfect original condition, its insurance replacement value would be five to eight times this auction price or value.

Item 14
"Jonah and the Whale" Pull Toy

What is it? Our Victorian ancestors wanted toys to teach valuable lessons by acting as learning tools. Many toys of the day had religious themes. This one, with its image of Jonah popping in and out of the whale's mouth, provided a wonderful visual aid to the familiar biblical story, and it is certain that no child who owned this toy would ever forget its particular cautionary tale.

This cast-iron pull toy was made by the N. N. Hill Brass Company of East Hampton, Connecticut, circa 1890. The company was founded by Norman N. Hill, who began learning about metal casting in the finishing department of the Barton Bell Company, which was founded in 1808 (East Hampton was known as "Bellville USA").

Valued at $588

Pull toy featuring image of "Jonah and the Whale." The whale has the name "Jonah" embossed on the side. The piece has a "cam" mechanism that causes the whale to swallow the figure of Jonah and then expel him. The figure of the whale rests on a pale blue wave-like base, which is supported by four wheels with spokes. The piece is 6 inches long, and has general rust and wear.

In 1889, Hill started his own bell company with very little capital, but it developed into what has been called the largest factory in the world, specializing in the making of toys, bells, and toys with bells. The firm was incorporated as the N. N. Hill Brass Company, Inc. in 1912 and continued to make toys well into the 1960s.

This cast-iron "Jonah and the Whale" pull toy is a wonderful example of N. N. Hill's work, but the company is probably best remembered for the toys made under the auspices of the Disney Company starting in the 1930s. They are especially known for their toy telephones that featured Disney characters.

What is it worth? This piece sold at auction in December 2004 for $588.

Item 15
Horse-Drawn Sleigh Toy

Valued at $1,870

Horse-drawn sleigh with a driver in a top hat. This cast-iron piece is 16 inches long by 6 inches high. A single wheel is attached to the horse's right rear leg. The figure of the driver is original, and the green sleigh has embossed decoration in gold. There is paint loss, but overall the paint is in good condition.

What is it? This charming sleigh brings back memories of winter scenes on Christmas cards and Currier and Ives prints. We can close our eyes and daydream a bit about simpler times and our ancestors gliding on a glistening blanket of snow—perhaps going to Grandmother's house for some sort of festive gathering.

This particular sleigh and driver was made circa 1911 by Dent Hardware Company of Fullerton, Pennsylvania. Henry H. Dent and four partners went into business manufacturing hardware items in 1895, but they did not begin producing cast-iron toys until several years later, around 1898.

Dent is known for its fine-quality vehicles such as fire trucks, dump trucks, buses, passenger cars, and police cars. They also made cast-iron cap pistols, airplanes, dirigibles, and steam shovels. In addition, Dent made a cast-iron version of the "Toonerville Trolley," a cartoon conveyance created by Fontaine Fox.

This comic strip first appeared in the *Chicago Post* in 1908, and continued to be published until 1955, when Fox retired. During its heyday in the 1930s, the strip, which was officially called *Toonerville Folks*, ran in at least 300 newspapers. The trolley was driven by Louie, the Skipper, and it was so endearing to readers with its temperamental and erratic behavior that many newspapers ran the comic strip as *Toonerville Trolley*. (An example of Dent's *Toonerville Trolley* in good condition in the box has an insurance replacement value of $1,750.)

In the 1920s, Dent was one of the first companies to try to cast toys from aluminum, but they had very little success with this line of products. During the hard times of the Great Depression in the 1930s, Dent stopped making toys.

What is it worth? This piece sold at auction in May 2004 for $1,870.

Item 16
Andy Gump Car

Valued at $1,045

Cast-iron car with red body and large disk wheels with whitewall tires. A figure in a hat sits at the steering wheel of the two-seater car. In addition, the car has a radiator cap and an engine crank, and the license plate has number 348 on it. The red paint on the body is fading, but otherwise, the surface is in good condition, with some paint flaking on the white portion of the tires.

What is it? How quickly we forget the "heroes" of the past. Today, few people could identify the person sitting in this roadster, but to newspaper readers of the 1920s, '30s, and '40s, there is no doubt that he represents Andy Gump.

This cartoon character first appeared in the *Chicago Tribune* in February 1917. Captain Joseph M. Patterson, editor/publisher of the *Tribune*, wanted a comic strip about the life of an ordinary family—people who were not particularly bright, wealthy, or physically attractive. The name Gump was chosen because to Patterson a "gump" was a member of the uneducated masses.

Sidney Smith was hired to draw and write the cartoon, and he developed Patterson's concept into a comic strip that captivated the American newspaper-reading public. There was Andy Gump, the chinless "poor lost soul," his wife, Min, their son, Chester, their maid, Tilda, and their wealthy Uncle Bim.

Within a few years, *Andy Gump* had achieved national distribution, and in 1931, Chicago's WGN launched an *Andy Gump* show, making it the first comic strip to become a radio show.

The show was extremely popular with listeners, and with this kind of national exposure came merchandising—everything from an *Andy Gump* song offered in sheet music (it was a fox trot, and the car pictured here was in the bottom right-hand corner of the cover) to a board game. A number of toys were also made, and the cast-iron example here was manufactured by the Arcade Manufacturing Company of Freeport, Illinois.

In 1885 a large foundry was opened in Freeport that made industrial casting and household items—but no toys. This company was incorporated as the Manufacturing Company, and in 1893, after a catastrophic fire, they began introducing cast-iron toys into their catalogs. These toys were so successful that by the early years of the 20th century, Arcade's toy catalog had grown to fifty pages.

Then a piece of serendipity happened. A lawyer, who had married the daughter of one of Arcade's directors, joined the firm in 1919. He happened to notice the large number of Yellow Cabs in the streets of Chicago, and he suggested to the company that they allow Arcade to manufacture models of their distinctive vehicles. Arcade got the right to make the toys, and Yellow Cab got the right to use the bright yellow vehicles for advertising purposes. (Other companies such as Dent made representations of the Yellow Cab as well.)

These were a tremendous success, and soon Arcade was making a wide variety of toy vehicles and farm equipment (tractors, corn planters, threshers, and combines, among others). These items were very successful, partially because they were true to the company's slogan "They Look Real."

The Great Depression and cut-rate competition put a great deal of pressure on Arcade, and in 1946, the company was sold to Rockwell Manufacturing Company of Pittsburgh, Pennsylvania. The Arcade plant in Freeport was subsequently closed when Rockwell moved its operation to Alabama.

As for Andy Gump, he and his family survived the death of Sidney Smith in 1935. The comic strip was taken over by Gus Edson, but slowly its popularity waned, and the merchandising ceased. By 1957, *Andy Gump* was published in just twenty newspapers, and in October of that year, the comic strip ceased publication.

What is it worth? This *Andy Gump* car sold at auction in May 2005 for $1,045.

Item 17
Vindex Truck

Valued at $5,500

Cast-iron truck with open bed and removable back lift gate. The piece is 7 1/2 inches long and painted dark green with nickel-colored wheels. On the truck bed is a hexagonal paper label that reads "Vindex Toys." There is chipping to the paint on both the truck and the wheels, but overall, the piece is in good to excellent condition.

What is it?

The maker of this toy is the Vindex Toys and Novelties Company of Belvedere, Illinois. This company has an interesting history and was part of the National Sewing Machine Company, which was formed in 1890 when the Eldredge Sewing Machine Company and the June Manufacturing Company joined together.

In the early 1900s, this company actually made some automobiles, but generally they specialized in making sewing machines for home use. Then, in 1928, they formed Vindex, which specialized in making high-quality cast-iron toys such as farm equipment, airplanes, still banks, and motorcycle toys, among others.

Both Hubley and Vindex tried to get the rights to make models of Harley-Davidson and Indian motorcycles, but Hubley made the deal and Vindex had to settle for making Excelsior-Henderson models. This company originally made bicycles, and made their first motorcycles in 1905. Later, it was bought out by Schwinn, which wanted to enter the motorcycle business.

Vindex reportedly made three Excelsior-Henderson models, two with "Mike the Speed Cop." One was of Mike alone, and the other was of Mike with his "captain" in a sidecar. The third piece was a motorcycle delivery cycle toy.

When they were new, Vindex toys were very expensive (some recent comments have referred to them as being "overpriced"), and there was resistance to buying them at retail. In response to this, Vindex offered them as premiums, and it is said that children would work very hard to earn the right to own a Vindex toy.

Unfortunately, Vindex was short lived and went out of business in 1932. As a result, and because their products were so expensive when they were new, Vindex toys in excellent condition are rare and often quite valuable.

What is it worth?

This Vindex open-bed truck sold at auction in May 2005 for $5,500.

Item 18

Buddy-L Truck

Valued at $1,600

Steel dump truck with black body, red chassis, and red disk wheels with silver rims. Buddy-L decal under the dashboard. The piece is 24 1/2 inches long with some paint wear and rust.

What is it? Fred Lundahl owned the Moline Pressed Steel Company of Moline, Illinois. He had a son named Arthur Brown Lundahl, but everyone called him Buddy L. Mr. Lundahl's main business, which was established around 1910, was making auto and truck parts such as fenders, but being a doting father, he began producing some pressed steel toys for his son.

These were very sturdy and could take the weight of a full-grown man standing on them. Buddy Lundahl's playmates liked the toys so much that their fathers began asking the senior Lundahl to make toys for their children as well. The result was the creation of Buddy "L" toys. The year was 1921.

Early Buddy "L" toys tend to be large and made from heavy-gauge steel. Starting in the early 1930s, however, the company began using lighter-weight materials. By this time, Fred Lundahl had passed away, but he had lost control of the company before then.

Over the years, the firm has been known as the Buddy "L" Corporation, the Buddy "L" Toy Company, and in more recent years the quotes have been dropped from around the "L." Quality and mate-

rials have changed as well; and during World War II it is reported that the company even made some wooden toys. In 2002, the Buddy L line was acquired by the Imperial Toy Corporation and is still being made today.

Buddy "L" made a great variety of toys, particularly trucks of every description (delivery trucks, street sprinkler trucks, oil trucks, ice trucks, and coal trucks, to name only a few) plus construction equipment (steam shovels, sand loaders, cranes, pile drivers, concrete mixers) and some highly prized electric trains. The piece pictured here appears to be the model 200A Hydraulic Dump Truck, which was manufactured between 1926 and 1931.

Due to the quality of the steel from which most Buddy "L" products were made, the toys tend to suffer from rust, corrosion, and loss of paint. Examples that are badly rusted or repainted bring much-reduced prices, but the piece here is in very good condition overall.

What is it worth? The insurance replacement value is $1,600.

TIN

Item 19

Painted Document Box

What is it? Describing this piece as being made from tin is something of a misnomer. It is actually tinplate, which means that it was made from thin sheets of iron or steel that had been coated in molten tin at a plating works. Tin is a silvery white metal used primarily to coat other metal to prevent corrosion and is part of numerous alloys, including pewter and bronze.

In the early days of the American colonies, tinplated items were imported. It was not until the beginning of the 18th century that production was begun on this side of the Atlantic, and then it was on a very small scale using tin imported from Great Britain. The actual American tinplate industry did not really begin in earnest until the early second quarter of the 19th century, circa 1830.

Tinplate was popular in American households because it was more sanitary and easily cleaned than wood. In addition, it was lighter than the iron used for kettles and cooking vessels, and it was cheaper than similar items made of either brass or copper.

Valued at $4,113

Covered box or document trunk, rectangular, with hinged domed lid, wire handle, and hasp for a lock. Height is 6 5/8 inches, width is 9 3/4 inches, and depth is 6 inches. The ground is black, with the body painted with a bird on a branch surrounded by flower blossoms, leaves, and buds in shades of red, green, and yellow. Around the lid, there is a spiral "S" band with dots, and the top and sides are decorated with yellow pinwheels and fanciful brushstrokes.

Some people refer to the unpainted variety of tin as the "poor man's silver."

American tinplate tended to be undecorated until the early years of the 19th century, when painting the surface became fashionable. Tinware was a necessity in most homes and farms, and it was made in a wide variety of shapes that ranged from milk pans and buckets to nursing bottles, coffeepots, cookie cutters, tea caddies, teapots, trays, and sugar bowls.

Tin was so important that the tenth wedding anniversary became the "tin anniversary" and married couples customarily exchanged gifts made from tin. Such curiosities as tin top hats and tin bonnets were made for this occasion, and these odd fripperies are now prized by collectors.

In addition, there was also a "tin wedding certificate" in which the couple celebrating ten years together were united in "tin-marriage," and on occasion, a tin document to that effect was made.

The lyric for P. P. Bliss's song "Tin Wedding" recounts how on this anniversary friends came by the couple's house and made a "clatter and a din" with tin trumpets and trays. This must have been a charming custom that has been lost in the modern world.

Document boxes or trunks like the one pictured here were a necessity for storing papers of importance that could range from wills and deeds to cherished love letters. The style of painting indicates this piece is thought to have been made by the Oliver Filley Tin Decorating Shop of Bloomfield (later Simsbury), Connecticut.

Filley was born in 1784 and was responsible for the family farm from the time his father died when he was just twelve years old. Around the year 1800, Filley left the farm to set himself up as a tinsmith (sometimes called a tin-knocker). Over the years, he was very successful, and there were a number of tinsmiths working in his shop. He also taught the trade to a number of his relatives, including his brother Harvey; his sons, Oliver Dwight Jr. and Lucius; and his cousin Augustus.

Members of the Filley family scattered to places such as Philadelphia, St, Louis, and Troy, New York, to set up businesses producing items made from tin. Oliver helped finance these moves, taught them the business aspects of the trade and helped them train decorators.

It seems probable that the wives of both Oliver Filley and his cousin Augustus were decorators of the tin that was made in the shop. This process often started with a "japan" finish, which was a layer of tar-based varnish that resembled paint to serve as a background. At the time of its invention it was intended to simulate the surface of Asian lacquer ware.

The first coat of this varnish was honey colored, but when layered and baked, it became black to bronze. Other colored backgrounds such as yellow and green were achieved by using oil-based paint. There was also a Prussian blue varnish that was used on rare occasions. The oil-based colors are prone to "alligatoring," which means that they can develop a network of cracks that resemble an alligator's hide.

Decorating the japanned surface was sometimes called "flowering," because the depiction of flowers was the common decoration for most American painted tinware. Pieces with images of leaves, acorns, and fruit rarely turn up, and the bird on this example makes it a very uncommon example.

It should be understood that scenic designs are generally not American but European in origin. French tinware, whether painted or unpainted, is properly called Tole or Toleware, but this term should never be applied to American pieces.

The condition of this document trunk is very good, with the sort of minor wear that is associated with day-to-day use of the fragile surface. There is no repainting, and collectors should beware of old pieces of tin that have new paint. In addition, painting on tin in the 19th-century style is a popular hobby and has been since at least the early 1900s. Be aware that most of the tin pieces encountered in the current marketplace have been either repainted or painted by a hobbyist in the early-20th century.

What is it worth? This box was sold at auction in June 2005 for $4,113.

Item 20
Lantern

Valued at $1,500

Lantern with eight sides. The frame is made from tin with arched glazed panels, and the dividers have finials and drops with similar feet. There is a ring handle at the top, and the three-tiered stepped chimney is decorated with crescent moon–shaped piercing. The piece is 21 1/2 inches tall.

What is it? Tin was a very important metal used in the crafting of early American lighting devices. Tin was used to make chandeliers, candleholders, sconces, and lanterns. Lanterns posed their own particular problems, because the flame had to be protected from the wind when in use outdoors or inside drafty barns. Yet the flame had to have a way to draw air so that it would have enough oxygen to keep burning brightly.

This meant that tin lanterns often had piercing over their entire surface and the light came through the holes—but this arrangement really cut down on the amount of illumination that could be emitted. These lanterns had the advantage of being able to take rough usage, because there was no glass to break.

To allow more light to show through a lantern, glass was sometimes used. But because glass was expensive, it was reserved for lanterns that might be on public view and not just the utilitarian object lighting the way in the utter darkness to the barn or outhouse. The rather decorative feet on the piece pictured here suggest that it might have been designed to be placed on a table from

time to time, just as the ring at the top indicates that it could also be easily hung. In fact, this piece may have been intended to be used as a hall lantern and hung from the ceiling in an entryway, and the glass protected the flame from being blown out every time the door was opened.

The piercings seen on this piece are part necessity and part decoration. They were made using a chisel and/or a punch that pierced holes in the metal when forcefully struck with a hammer. To make ornamentation on tin that was purely decorative a punch was used to make a raised "dot" or line on the outside surface that did not go all the way through the metal. These "dots" or raised "dimples" could be arranged to form dates, names, and/or geometric designs.

This lantern is probably from the second quarter of the 19th century.

What is it worth? This piece sold at auction in August 2005 for $1,500.

Tin coffeepot approximately 11 1/4 inches tall with a domed lid that has a brass finial. It has an applied strap handle and a hooked spout. The background is black with a yellowed white band around the rim, which has been painted with red fruit and green leaves. The body is painted with red, yellow, and white painted flowers and fruit with a yellow-and-white brushstroke border. The piece has expected wear and losses.

What is it?

Coffee was never made in a pot such as this one because the heat of the flames would have destroyed the attractive decoration. Instead, the coffee was brewed in an undecorated vessel and then transferred to this one to be served to guests.

Some of these decorated pots have dark rims around the bottom that suggest they have been exposed to heat sometime in the past. This kind of damage may have happened when the pot was put on the fire to rewarm the coffee quickly after it had been in the pot for a while. The person responsible for this was probably in a hurry and did not want to go through the hassle of transferring the tepid liquid from the fancy pot to the utilitarian one just for a quick warmup.

American tin coffeepots from the early 19th century took several forms. Some had straight spouts that met the body at an acute angle, some had curved spouts that are vaguely reminiscent of those found on an oil can, while others had the characteristic hook shape seen on the example pictured here.

The overall shape of this coffeepot is called a "lighthouse" because its tall cylindrical profile resembles one of those seashore towers with a light on top. The body of this piece was probably made from a standard sheet of tin that was ten by fourteen inches. This flat piece of metal was subsequently hand shaped using simple tools such as wooden mallets, chisels, tin snips, and soldering irons.

The "tin-knocker" who made this coffeepot probably did so at a wooden bench that had a charcoal brazier close by on which he melted the tin that he used as solder. In all likelihood, the tinsmith had tin templates to guide him as he cut out the forms that were joined together to make up this pot. He would put the seams together using solder—or perhaps he would roll the edges of the two sides that he wanted to join and hook them before hammering them tightly together against the anvil or "stake." Some outside edges were merely folded over, while others were rolled over wire to give added strength.

What is it worth?

Sold at auction in 2006, this early 19th century tinplate coffeepot from New England brought $2,350.

Item 21
Candle Sconces

Valued at $6,500

Tin candle sconces with long rectangular back plates topped with a foliate design. "D"-shaped trays at the bottom hold a single candle, and the back is decorated with a starflower at the point where there is a small hole that was used to attach these sconces to the wall. They are 19 inches tall.

What is it?

This is an exceptional pair of candle sconces attributed to Nelson Garey (1820–1910) of Berlin, Pennsylvania. Sconces are wall-hung candleholders that traditionally were used in the more formal rooms in homes—particularly parlors, dining rooms, and ballrooms—and in public rooms such as courtrooms and churches.

Sconces came in a wide variety of shapes and sizes, but one of their main attributes was that they needed to have a back that both protected the wall from the candle flame and had a bright surface that would reflect the candlelight, providing more light for the room. Some of these were shaped like round pie plates and had pieces of mirror attached to the back to act as more efficient reflectors, whereas others were more oval and relied on the polished surface of the tin to amplify the light.

Nelson Garey was born in Berlin, Pennsylvania, in 1820 and died in 1910. Garey apprenticed in the tin trade for five years with Phineas Compton of Salisbury, Pennsylvania, and then worked in several places before becoming foreman of a tinshop in Cumberland, Pennsylvania. He returned to Berlin in 1850, married, set up his own shop, and remained in Berlin until his death.

Garey used a template to make his sconces with red oak leaf tops, and a famous pair of his sconces are in Delaware's Winterthur Museum. This image of the leaves is quite well done, with the edges intricately cut out and the details of the leaf correct right down to the veining that radiates from the center line just as it would in a real leaf.

The punched starflower suggests Pennsylvania Dutch or Moravian influence. The shiny surface of the tin is largely gone on these pieces and was probably polished away over the years in a vain attempt to keep the surface reflective. Now what is left is basically the underlying iron, which has some corrosion. These sconces attributed to Nelson Garey should be dated to the third quarter of the 19th century.

What is it worth?

This pair of sconces sold at auction in August 2005 for $6,500.

Item 22
Quatrefoil Candle Sconces

Valued at $1,500

Pair of tin sconces with quatrefoil-shaped back plates and single candle cups in rectangular drip pans. The edges of these pieces have been crimped, and the back plates are pierced for hanging. They are 15 1/2 inches tall.

What is it?

Prior to the end of the 18th century, tinware was made exclusively by hand. But then the Industrial Revolution brought machinery into the lives of craftsmen on both sides of the Atlantic. Populations were growing. The demand for household goods was increasing, and the technology was available to find machines that could make production easier and quicker.

There is a story that tinsmith Eli Parsons and his wife were attending church services one Sunday in Dedham, Massachusetts, when Eli suddenly propelled himself from his pew yelling, "I've got it! I've got it!" We are sure that Eli's wife, Abigail, must have feared that he had suddenly developed some sort of terrible mental aberration, but what he had actually gotten was a notion about how to make a number of machines that would make his job easier and improve his production.

Parsons and Calvin Whiting formed a partnership, and early in 1804 they patented a number of machines that could be used to cut and shape tin. One machine was rolling shears that would cut sheet tin. Another was a Sweep Gage that would hold tin plates while they were cut into circular form, and still another was for locking the sides of a tin vessel together.

Among the gadgets in this original patent, there was not a machine that would crimp edges for decorative purposes, but such a machine was invented, and its work can be seen along the edges of this pair of sconces. The precision and regularity of the parallel grooves say "machine made," but the pieces were assembled by hand.

It is a bit hard to imagine how these would have looked when they were first made, but the surface would have been very bright to reflect light. However, attempting to restore the surface now would be a tragedy and would greatly detract from the monetary value of these fine 19th-century tin sconces because serious collectors prefer an original patina on their tinware.

What is it worth?

This pair sold at auction in August 2005 for $1,500.

Item 23
Chandelier

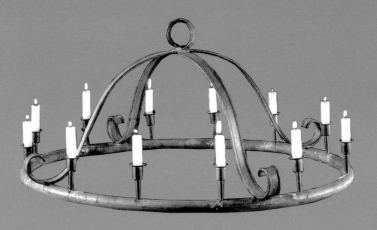

Valued at $25,000

Chandelier, oval, 24 by 34 inches.
The oval ring is hickory that has been
painted gray-green, and it in turn
supports twelve single candleholders
made from pewter and tin. This ring
is attached to an arched "X"-form strap
work terminating in simple scrolls.
In the center is a ring for suspending
the chandelier from the ceiling.

What is it? As a general rule, this is not the sort of lighting device associated with a private home. Instead, this is a piece that might be found in a variety of public buildings or institutions.

To be sure, twelve candles would not give off enough light to illuminate a large room such as a dining hall or a tavern taproom. This chandelier, however, has a provenance that suggests that it was once one of a pair that hung in the Linden Hall School for Girls, which was founded by the Moravians in Lititz, Pennsylvania, in 1746. This boarding school is just seven miles outside Lancaster, Pennsylvania and is still in operation.

The mate to this piece was a gift from Titus Geesey to the Philadelphia Museum of Art and is illustrated in their *Pennsylvania German Collection* (page 54). This type of provenance and connection to a prestigious collection is of great interest to collectors and greatly increases the monetary value of this chandelier.

What is it worth? This chandelier with its fine provenance sold at auction in August 2005 for $25,000.

Item 24
Drugstore Sign

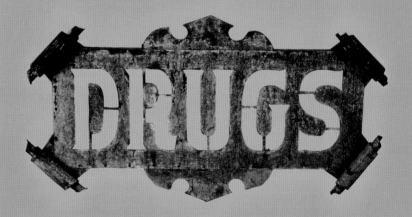

Valued at $1,763

Sign with scrolled corners, tin face
mounted to a wooden frame. The piece is
54 inches long by 18 1/4 inches tall. The
word "DRUGS" has been cut through the
tin, and there are vestiges of old paint
that is much weathered.

What is it? This charming sign once hung outside a pharmacy to attract the attention of passing customers and mark the spot along a busy downtown street where drugs and sundries—and perhaps a refreshing soft drink or ice-cream cone—could be purchased. This particular sign is circa 1900.

In this day of signs that pulse with neon flashes or overwhelm with bright paint and huge sizes, this sign is refreshingly stylish but nonintrusive. It speaks of simpler times, stores that were not mega-chains in strip malls littered around the country, and establishments where the proprietor knew the name of his customers and cared about his or her needs. In other words, the charm and appeal of this sign is largely in its nostalgia and in its ability to take us back to earlier, perhaps less complicated days.

The sign is also appealing to collectors because it was handmade by a craftsman who shaped and curled the corners of the edges in a most attractive way, and then cut out the letters so that they appear to have been made using a stencil as a guide. Signs such as this one make great decorations today, and they preserve our material heritage.

Collectors are interested in a wide variety of signs. Some like the ones that feature iconic brands such as Coca-Cola, and some like those made in the shape of a particular object such as a shoe or a pair of eyeglasses that symbolized the nature of the establishment being advertised. Pharmacies often had signs featuring the representation of a mortar and pestle, and the departure from this typical image for this example is very engaging.

What is it worth? This tin pharmacy sign sold at auction in February 2001 for $1,763.

Item 25
"Tintype" Photograph

Valued at $650

Photographic image on a metal plate made of iron. The piece is 7 3/4 inches by 10 inches and has a picture of a man sitting in a chair with a crutch. On the back is scratched "Sgt. Walker Gettysburg Veteran." There is some hand coloring on the rug. The top two corners are bent, and there is some crackling to the surface that is visible only under good light.

What is it?

Photographs such as this one have two names. The one popularly used is "tintype," but the more correct nomenclature is "ferrotype." The former piece of nomenclature might indicate to some that this photograph is on a piece of tin, but it is not. It is actually on a thin iron plate, and this is indicated by the suffix "ferro," which means "iron."

There was some debate as to whether or not this item belonged in the section on tin or the one on iron. The tin section finally prevailed because "tintype" is the name most often applied to this type of photograph by casual collectors and laymen.

"Tintypes" are one-of-a-kind photographs that are sometimes called the "poor man's daguerreotype." Generally, they are of much less interest to collectors than daguerreotypes, which were made on thick copper plates and have a very distinctive mirror-like finish.

Tintypes were invented in 1856 by Hamilton Smith, a professor of chemistry in Ohio. In this process, the photograph was created on a thin iron plate that was coated with a black japan varnish. These were made in fairly large quantities until the turn of the 20th century, and even at a distance they can be distinguished by their dark surface with no mirror-like sheen.

Pre-1865 tintypes are often found in cases, but cardboard holders replaced these in the late 1860s and finally they were placed in nothing at all. Early tintypes are black and white, but ones made after about 1870 often have a brown tone. Sometimes, tintypes are found embellished with a little hand coloring such as the example shown here.

This is an oversized piece, because a whole or full plate is usually only 6 1/2 by 8 1/2 inches (see the discussion of daguerreotypes in item #40, page 109). This example is somewhat larger than that, and the bigger format contributes to the photograph's rarity and desirability to collectors.

In addition, the subject matter of this tintype is much in its favor because pieces associated with the Civil War are sought by collectors, as are pieces in which the subject of the photograph is identified. To be sure, collectors generally prefer Civil War portraits to have been made during the time of the conflict and to feature soldiers in full uniform with guns, swords, and appropriate accouterments—the more the better.

This particular "tintype" was made after the conflict circa 1870, the subject of the portrait is not in uniform, and his only accoutrement is his crutch, which was earned at Gettysburg. The photo actually has two serious problems: the bent corners and the crazing to the finish. In many cases, tintypes that have these problems are worth little or nothing, but in this case, they do not detract from the aesthetic merits of the photograph.

What is it worth? The insurance replacement value is $650.

 (Note: Many small tintypes with portraits of ordinary, unidentified subjects are worth less than $10 each.)

Item 26
Popeye with Punching Bag

What is it? Popeye the Sailor (King Features) first appeared in Elzie Segar's *Thimble Theater* comic strip on January 17, 1929. This comic revolved around the Oyl family—including Olive Oyl and her brother, Castor Oyl.

For this first strip, Popeye was little more than a walk-on character of little importance. In this piece, Castor Oyl and his friend Ham Gravy need transportation for an overseas trip. They go down to the docks and spot a sailor and ask, "Hey there! Are you a sailor?" only to have Popeye reply, "Ja think I'm a cowboy?"

Popeye soon became an important part of *Thimble Theater*, and within a year, the character of Ham Gravy was gone and Popeye was Olive Oyl's boyfriend. J. Wellington Wimpy and his obsession with hamburgers was added in 1932, and Swee'Pea followed in 1936.

Valued at $990

Lithographed tin toy with a figure of Popeye with a punching bag. The punching bag is made from celluloid and supported on a wire. This toy has a clockwork mechanism and stands 7 1/2 inches tall. There is no box, but the surface is in very good condition except for some rubbed places at the corners of the green base.

Popeye made his first appearance in an animated cartoon in 1933 when he was featured in *Betty Boop Meets Popeye the Sailor*, and over the years that followed, he appeared in approximately 750 other animated features. Over the years, Popeye has become an icon, and many products (including canned spinach available in grocery stores) have used his name and image.

This particular Popeye toy was manufactured by the Chein Company, which began in a loft in New York City in 1903. The founder was Julius Chein (pronounced "chain"), and initially the company was a metal-stamping operation that made tin prizes to be placed in Cracker Jack boxes and other small tin toys that were sold in five-and-dime stores.

In 1907, Chein opened a plant in Harrison, New Jersey, to manufacture lithographed tin toys. The company prospered and obtained the rights to make toys featuring the image of Popeye, Felix the Cat, various Disney characters, and later the Mutant Ninja Turtles. During World War II, however, Chein made munitions as well as nose cones and tails for bombs to aid the war effort.

After the war, the competition from Japanese lithographed tin toys was fierce, and Chein specialized in making larger ones that would be too bulky to be shipped economically from the Far East. In 1949, the company opened a larger facility in Burlington, New Jersey, and as the 20th century progressed, they made such items as lithographed tin wastebaskets, canister sets, and bread boxes in their housewares division.

Ultimately, child safety issues and the cost of steel took Chein out of the toy business. In the 1980s the company was sold to Atlantic Can Company and became Atlantic Cheinco Corporation. They went bankrupt in 1992.

The Chein Company had a special relationship with Woolworth's, who carried their toys almost exclusively. The Popeye with a punching bag pictured above is from the second quarter of the 20th century.

What is it worth? This Chein lithographed tin toy featuring Popeye with a punching bag was sold in May 2005 for $990.

Related item

Lithographed tin toy representing Popeye with an overhead punching bag. The figure stands on a square base and has a circular canopy overhead from which is suspended a celluloid representation of a punching bag. The piece has a clockwork mechanism and stands 9 1/2 inches tall. It has its original box, which is signed "J. Chein Company Harrison, New Jersey." The toy itself is in near mint condition, but the box has some tears and pieces missing.

What is it?

Both Popeye and the Chein Company were discussed previously, but this particular piece is shown to demonstrate the difference that little details can make in a toy's value. This toy and the toy before are very similar and show Popeye (King Features) with a punching bag. One is mounted on the base, and the other bag is suspended from a canopy over Popeye's head.

Despite the similarities, the Chein Popeye with overhead punching bag shown here is more than six times more valuable than the one with the base-mounted bag featured in the previous section. Why?

The example pictured here is in much better condition than the previous Popeye with the base-mounted punching bag and has its original box while the other does not. In addition, the colorful lithograph on the Popeye with the overhead punching bag is far more interesting than that found on the previous piece. Lastly, this toy is somewhat rarer and harder to find than the simpler Popeye with the base-mounted punching bag.

Not one of the factors outlined above accounts for the huge difference in price, but all taken together do. Collectors can be very picky and judgmental, but this is a good thing and really what collecting is all about—separating the rare from the not so rare and prizing pieces that have survived the years in great to pristine condition over other examples that have not been so fortunate.

What is it worth?

This Popeye with the overhead punching bag sold at auction in May 2005 for $6,050.

Item 27

Mickey and Minnie Mouse Washing Machine

What is it? Walt Disney's Mickey and Minnie Mouse need no introduction—at least not to anyone who has been near a toy store, theater, television set, or certain amusement parks scattered around the globe.

Mickey was the creation of Walt Disney and Ub Iwerks, and this rambunctious anthropomorphic mouse first appeared in *Steamboat Willie*, which was first shown at the Colony Theater in New York City on November 18, 1928. With Mickey in this first animated cartoon, which was also the first cartoon with synchronized sound, was Mickey's girlfriend Minnie Mouse, also known as Minerva Mouse.

In that first cartoon, Mickey serenades Minnie by playing "Turkey in the Straw" using a bevy of animal instruments. Initially, Mickey did not speak but made noises and squeaks, voiced by Walt Disney himself.

Mickey did not actually speak until *The Karnival Kid*, which debuted May 23, 1929—and again Walt Disney supplied the characteristic voice. Disney continued being the voice of Mickey Mouse until 1946, when Jim McDonald took over. McDonald filled this role until 1983, when Wayne Allwine became the voice of Mickey.

Valued at $2,090

Lithographed tin washing machine featuring images of Mickey and Minnie Mouse washing their clothes. The piece is 7 3/4 inches tall and is in near mint condition. It has its original box, which has been restored.

Mickey and Minnie may both be mice, but they have also been "cash cows" for Disney. The outpouring of Mickey Mouse–theme merchandise has been unprecedented. Many companies made Mickey Mouse–themed toys, and one of them was the Ohio Art Company of Bryan, Ohio, which made the whimsical washing machine shown above.

Ohio Art was founded in 1908, and today, they are probably best known for their Etch-A-Sketch and a rubber doll called Betty Spaghetty. The founder of the company was H. S. Winzeler, a dentist whose original plan was to manufacture metal picture frames. In 1917, he bought the C. E. Carter Erie Toy Plant and started making lithographed tin toys.

Later, this facility was sold to Louis Marx, but Ohio Art continued to make lithographed tin toys and is still very much in business today.

What is it worth? This Ohio Art Company Mickey and Minnie Mouse washing machine sold at auction in May 2005 for $2,090.

PEWTER

Item 28

Thomas D. and Sherman Boardman Flagon

What is it? Pewter is an alloy of tin and copper that some-times has other metals such as bismuth, antimony, and lead added to the mixture. When the first English colonists came to America, they brought their molds to make pewter, and the early pewter made on these shores looks exactly like the pewter that was being made across the Atlantic at the same time.

American-made pieces, however, are far more desirable and valuable (at least in the United States) than the British exam-ples they so closely resemble. In most cases, only the marks found on the bottom or back can distinguish the two, and for this reason pewter collectors often display their plates and plat-ters with the backs facing out so the all-important marks are on view. It should be mentioned that the vast majority of genuine

Valued at $3,819

Tall tankard flagon, 3-quart capacity, with urn-shaped finial on a domed and molded cover with "chairback" thumbpiece atop a double-scrolled handle with a bud-shaped terminal. It is 14 inches tall, and the body is a tapered cylinder with molded fillet and base. On the bottom is the mark "TD & SB" with an eagle and an "X."

American antique pewter is marked on the underside and not on the front or side. One exception to this is the 8-inch plates made by Samuel Hamlin of Providence, Rhode Island, who marked his pieces in the plate's well.

For many of our 17th-, 18th-, and early-19th-century ancestors, silver vessels and utensils were just too expensive, and they had to settle for items made from either wood or pewter. Well-made pewter crafted from the highest-quality metal had a beautiful surface similar to silver. Generally speaking, the more silvery the metal, the better quality the pewter, and the darker the metal, the lower the quality of the pewter.

Early American pewterers made all sorts of items from spoons and plates to large oval platters called boar's-head platters and open tankard mugs that are often called pots. They also made such things as measures, dishes, basins, porringers, lidded tankards, beakers, ladles, and flagons similar to the one pictured here.

Flagons were traditionally used in churches for ecclesiastical purposes. They were often made in sets that consisted of a flagon

American Metalware   77

Mark used by Sherman and
Thomas Boardman

such as this one for holding communion wine; cups, chalices, or beakers from which the communion wine was drunk by the parishioners; 6-inch-diameter plates or "patens" for holding the communion bread; a baptismal basin; and several dishes that generally had a diameter ranging from 11 to 13 inches.

More prosperous churches had these ecclesiastical sets in silver, but country congregations often used pewter vessels, and it was customary for these items to be gifts to the church from prosperous members of the congregation. Often, these sets were assembled over a period of time with individual pieces made by several different makers. This particular piece was made in Hartford, Connecticut, by Thomas D. and Sherman Boardman and is circa 1815–20.

Thomas Danforth Boardman was born in Litchfield, Connecticut, in 1784, but moved to Hartford in 1795. In 1796 at age twelve, he began an apprenticeship with his uncle Edward Danforth, who was a member of the famous Danforth family of pewterers that had done business in Taunton, Massachusetts, since 1727. In 1799, he continued his training with Samuel Danforth, Edward's younger brother.

According to Boardman's diary, he set up his own business on July 21, 1804, at the age of twenty years and six months. It is said that Thomas Boardman may have been the first person in the United States to make Britannia metal. He says in his notes that in 1806 he added "2 or 3 per ct. copper ... and as much R antimony (Regulus of antimony)" to tin to make the variety of pewter that became so important to makers of electroplated silver later in the 19th century. He further states that the Boardman firm kept this process a secret until 1821.

Sherman Boardman, Thomas Boardman's partner, was born in 1787 and died in 1861. About 1810, this duo formed the partnership whose mark appears on the base of this beautiful flagon.

What is it worth? Flagons are highly desired by pewter collectors, and this example sold at auction in June 2004 for $3,819.

Item 29
Thomas Danforth III Dish

Valued at $1,645

Pewter dish 6 1/4 inches diameter and marked with a Federal-style eagle set in a circular serrated reserve with rays around its head, holding a shield and clutching an olive branch in one talon and arrows in the other. This is the only mark, and there are no names or initials.

What is it?

Pewter making was often a family business, and many times, members of a familial grouping were involved in this industry for generation after generation. The distinctive eagle mark on the piece pictured here identifies the maker of this deep bowl as Thomas Danforth III, of the famous Danforth family mentioned in connection with the flagon in the preceding section.

The Danforth dynasty of pewterers was founded by Thomas Danforth the first (1793–86), and he is reportedly the first person to make pewter in Connecticut. Danforth opened his first shop in Taunton, Massachusetts, in 1727, but in 1733, he relocated and began a pewter-making operation in Norwich, Connecticut. Thomas was married twice and had a total of fourteen children. Two of them, Thomas II (1731–82) and John (1741–99) became pewterers in their own right.

Thomas II apprenticed under his father, and after finishing his training, moved to Middleton, Connecticut, where he set up his own pewter-making shop. During the Revolutionary War, Thomas II made musket balls for the Continental Army. It should be noted that much of the pre–Revolutionary War pewter made in this country was melted down and turned into musket balls during this conflict, which makes pre-1770s American pewter very rare indeed.

Thomas II had five sons who became pewterers, and his eldest, Thomas III (1756–1840) made the circa 1790 plate pictured above. Thomas III is considered to be the Danforth pewterer with the largest trade, and the one who made the highest-quality product. In 1777, during the opening years of the Revolutionary War, he opened his own shop in Stepney (now called Rocky Hill) Connecticut; in addition to pewter, he made objects from copper, tin, and brass.

In 1807, Thomas III opened a second shop in Philadelphia, where he made vast quantities of pewter that have survived to this day. Despite the fact that the Philadelphia operation was highly successful, Thomas III shut down the facility in 1813 and returned to Rocky Hill, where he reportedly retired in 1818.

Thomas Danforth III used several marks during his career, but the eagle without his initials was first used circa 1790, and this mark is considered to be rare. An eagle insignia with his "T D" initial obscuring the talons, olive branch, and arrows first appeared about 1800.

What is it worth?

The work of Thomas Danforth III is highly regarded by collectors, and this example sold at auction in June 2004 for $1,645.

Item 30
Samuel Hamlin Quart Mug

Valued at $1,058

Pewter quart mug, signed "Samuel Hamlin" on the bottom. It is 5 7/8 inches tall with a cylindrical form. There is an everted (turned outward) lip, a molded fillet, a molded base, and an "S" scroll handle with bud terminal. There is some wear.

Mark used by
Thomas
Danforth III

What is it? In the 17th and 18th centuries the main forms of pewter hollowware were the covered tankard, the measure, and the uncovered mug, which was referred to as a "pot" in many inventories of the period. Of this group, the covered tankard was the aristocrat, and is today one of the most desired forms for modern collectors.

While the tankard had a place on the tables of the rich, the open mug was found on the tables of the less well-to-do and in taverns. These were widely made in pint and quart sizes (thus the old saying "Mind your "P's" and "Q's"—for pints and quarts, which were sometimes marked with either a "p" or a "q").

Samuel Hamlin was born September 9, 1746, in Middletown, Connecticut, and according to tradition, was apprenticed in the shop of Thomas Danforth II. In 1769, young Hamlin went into partnership with Benjamin Henshaw. As reported in the *Connecticut Courant* of July 13, 1767, he began doing business at the shop of Widow Hooker, where they made a variety of items in brass and pewter that they sold for cash, "country produce," or for old pewter, brass, copper, or lead.

How long this partnership lasted is a bit vague, but it is reported that Hamlin married in 1771 and moved shortly thereafter to Providence, Rhode Island, where he set up shop at the head of Long Wharf as a pewterer, brazier (or brass worker), and coppersmith. In 1774, Hamlin had a son, Samuel Ely Hamlin, who eventually apprenticed in his father's shop and took over at the elder Hamlin's death in 1801.

The younger Hamlin continued to use his father's marks and molds for a period of time, and it is sometimes hard to distinguish the work of the father from that of the son by using the evidence of marks and forms. The younger Hamlin worked until 1856 (he died in 1864), and in the latter years he worked in Britannia metal. Samuel E. Hamlin is known for maintaining the quality of his father's work even into the Britannia era.

The quart pot or mug pictured on the preceding page was made by the senior Hamlin circa 1790.

What is it worth? Pewter mugs of the late 18th and early 19th century made by quality pewterers are hard, but not impossible, to find. This one sold at auction in 2004 for $1,058.

Item 31
Hasselberg Group Plate

Valued at $250
Pewter plate, 9 5/8 inches in diameter.
This plate was much used and has
a small hole in the metal and a
rectangular patch on the reverse side.
It is marked with a crown over an "X"
with a round mark with two love
birds below a crown. The front has
a crest consisting of a crown with a
fish emerging from the top.

What is it?

The various marks found on the back of this plate associate it with what has been called the Hasselberg Group of Philadelphia, Pennsylvania. The group consisted of Abraham Hasselberg, who was of Swedish derivation; John Adam Koehler, who married Hasselberg's widow; and John A. Brunstrom, who married Hasselberg's daughter.

Hasselberg learned the pewtering trade in Norrkoping, Sweden, and was a journeyman in Stockholm. He is recorded as having worked in Sweden from about 1735 to 1745 or so. The years 1745 to 1749 are a bit of a blank in the Hasselberg history, but in 1750, he sailed from London with members of the United Brethren to join the Moravian community established by Count Zinsendorf at Bethlehem, Pennsylvania.

By the late 1750s (the date is uncertain), Hasselberg had left the Moravian colony and was working in Wilmington, Delaware. In 1759, he advertised in Wilmington that he was a pewterer and tinman, but by 1762, he had left Wilmington and had moved to nearby Philadelphia.

Hasselberg died in 1779, and in 1780 his widow married John Adam Koehler, a deserter from the British army. Koehler had taken the Oath of Allegiance in 1779 to the new United States, and continued Abraham Hasselberg's pewter business. Then, in 1783, John A. Brunstrom entered the picture when he married the Hasselberg daughter, and the pewter business apparently passed to him from his wife's stepfather.

The origin of the love bird mark (sometimes called the "love touch") on this piece is open to some conjecture. Some sources say the mark is that of John A. Brunstrom, whereas others say it is a symbol associated with the Moravian community in Bethlehem, and that Hasselberg may have used it and then taken it with him when he left and continued to use it for years. It is also speculated that after Hasselberg's death his descendants continued to use the "love touch." No one really knows for sure. The "X" over the crown is a quality mark associated with Sweden and pewterers of Swedish derivation.

Any piece of pewter that is less than 10 inches in diameter is termed a plate, and examples with a diameter larger than 10 inches are called dishes. It does not matter how deep the item's well happens to be, and a shallow piece more than 10 inches in diameter is still termed a dish, and a piece with a deep well might be termed a deep dish.

Most American pewter plates of the 18th century are circular with medium-width rims and a single reeding around the edges like the example pictured here. The diameters vary widely, but 8- and 9-inch examples are most common, and one at 9 5/8 inches in diameter is a bit unusual.

What is it worth?
Despite the interest of the marks and the history that is connected to them, pewter pieces with the Lovebird mark are relatively plentiful. This example should be valued for insurance replacement purposes for $250.

COPPER, BRONZE, AND MIXED METALS

Item 32
George Washington Inaugural Button

What is it? Today, we are accustomed to a barrage of campaign memorabilia every time there is a presidential election, but in the early days of our republic, this sort of memorabilia was very rare indeed.

At the time of George Washington's inauguration as the first president of the United States in 1789, there was an outpouring of commemorative and celebratory buttons that were designed to be worn on clothing—primarily men's coats, capes, and "breeches" (i.e., pants). It is thought that the large-size buttons were for coats, the medium size for capes, and the small size for breeches.

These items were crafted by New York and Connecticut button makers. In response to the examples sent to him by General Henry Knox, Washington referred to their quality by writing, "... they really do credit to the manufacturers of this Country." Originally, the buttons had shanks on the back so that they could be worn as clothing buttons, but many 19th-century collectors removed these shanks so that the medals would fit more easily (and flatly) into a display case.

These buttons came in a large variety of styles. Two of the most commonly found examples have the initials "GW" in an oval

Valued at $5,000

Button, 1 5/16 inches in diameter with the image of an eagle in the center with a sunburst over its head. There is a shield in the center of the eagle's chest, and one talon is clutching arrows while the other holds an olive branch. Around the outside is the inscription "MARCH THE FOURTH 1789 MEMORABLE ERA." The metal is copper that was once gilded. The gilding is now badly worn.

medallion in the center with the inscription "Long Live the President" around the top. There is also the so-called "Eagle and Star" button that is decorated with just an eagle and stars and no inscription.

Two favorites with collectors are the "Memorable Era" button pictured here, and the examples that have a chain of thirteen linked states surrounding a script "GW." Perhaps the rarest of all the George Washington inaugural buttons are the ones called the "Pater Patriae" or "Father of His Country" button. This is the only button to have a portrait of Washington on it, with the inscription "General Washington" above the picture of his head in a tricorn hat and "Pater Patriae" below.

Reproductions of these George Washington inauguration buttons exist in large numbers, and some other varieties are of questionable age. Separating the real from the fake requires knowledge and experience with genuine specimens.

What is it worth? Rare examples of George Washington inauguration buttons can bring close to $25,000 at auction. Examples of "Memorable Era" buttons can be found in both copper and brass, but authentic pieces should be valued at $5,000 in this condition.

Item 33
Gorham Mixed Metals Bowl

Valued at $1,400

Ovoid bowl with scalloped top and hand-hammered surface made from copper. The piece is decorated in relief with applied silver and copper to form the image of a branch with leaves and fruit. It is 3 1/2 inches high and marked with an anchor, "Gorham Co.," a style number, and an "O."

What is it? Gorham craftsmen made many pieces in the Asian style known as "Chinoiserie," which is primarily a Western adaptation of Chinese designs. However, these artisans were even more fascinated with Japanese designs on metalware that began finding their way to this country after Admiral Perry's 1854 treaty with Japan.

In the late 1860s Japanese life was in great turmoil. The Civil War of 1868 led to the abolition of feudalism in 1871. After these events, the Samurai were no longer allowed to carry swords, and some magnificent metalwares decorated with mixed metals such as gold, silver, bronze, and a number of alloys came onto the marketplace.

In its library, Gorham had a number of books on Japanese art, and Gorham artisans often took images from wood-block prints and incorporated them into their designs. During the 1870s and 1880s these Japanese influences were very strong, and some beautiful pieces were made in the Japanese or Japonaise taste.

It is possible, for example, to find ivory cups adorned with Gorham silver birds, dragons, trees, and/or insects; or iron tea caddies decorated with an applied silver dragon on the side and the three-dimensional image of a crab on the top. There are also tea sets with dragon handles made from red-enameled copper that have been embellished with silver and copper leaves and berries depicting cherry and plum blossoms.

Many of these pieces, including the example pictured here, appear to have hand-hammered surfaces, but there is more than one way to create this look. The idea of producing and leaving bold hammer marks on the surface of a piece of silver or copper appears to have originated at Tiffany around 1876 and been adopted at Gorham soon thereafter. These marks indicate that a piece has been hand formed, and communicate the idea of hand craftsmanship to many modern collectors.

One way to produce these marks is with a silversmith's hammer. This is done by placing the metal to be formed against an anvil or a stake (an iron anvil or tongue) and hitting it with the hammer in such a way as to produce the desired shape. Objects formed in this manner have smooth inside walls.

The other way to produce these marks is to use chasing tools. When this is done, the object is filled with pitch, which gives when the chasing tool strikes the surface. This in turn leaves visible marks on the inside walls, which are easily discernable with the eyes or the fingertips.

Hand hammering became more and more popular as the 19th century wore on into the 20th century, and Arts and Crafts metalware of this later period is often characterized by this hand-hammered look. This particular piece is an example of the American Aesthetic Movement, which took much of its design elements from Japanese and other Asian art.

In furniture, these Japanese elements were artistically applied to rectangular Eastlake forms. In the decorative arts, the pieces often looked to the untutored as if they might have been made in Japan, but they generally incorporated some Western design elements. In the piece under discussion here, the Japanese influence is seen in the use of the mixed metals and in the naturalism of the subject matter, but the fruiting plants themselves are more of a Western representation.

Maintaining the original finish on the surface of metal pieces such as this one is very important, and polishing should be avoided. There is no problem with polishing the silver as long as it is done carefully so as not to remove details that were placed there in the making, such as gilding or areas of oxidation that were applied by the maker to enhance the design.

Copper and bronze surfaces on decorative objects, however, should not be polished for any reason. This small ovoid bowl has its original surface, and that is much in its favor. The "O" found in the mark indicates that this piece was made by Gorham in 1882.

What is it worth? The insurance replacement value is $1,400.

Related item

The lamp base that has been converted from kerosene to electricity is made from patinated copper with mixed metal accents. It is 14 inches tall with a rectangular cubic body that has three-dimensional heads of Buddhist lions on either side. Above the rectangular body there is a die-rolled silver band around a cylinder form that supports a single electric socket with a pull chain. Around the base are scroll and leaf overlays that terminate in paw feet. The base has been drilled through to allow for the electrical cord. It is marked with an anchor, "Gorham Co.," and a boar's head.

What is it?

This lamp base is a blending of styles, with the Buddhist lions being largely of Chinese derivation while the bands around the cylinder are more in the Islamic tradition. The piece was made by Gorham in 1885 and has a boar's-head date mark. Gorham used letter symbols "A" through "Q" from 1868 to 1884, but in 1885 they used a figure as a symbol for the first time—a boar's head.

The big issue with this lamp base is the electrification. There is no question that the socket itself is ugly and distracts from the overall beauty of the base, but the real problem is that the base has been pierced. Collectors of lamps do not care if a lamp has been electrified as long as it can be returned to its original state with no harm. Unfortunately, the integrity of this lamp was violated when it was converted, and it cannot be easily returned to its original condition.

Many purist collectors will reject a lamp that has had its font (kerosene reservoir) punctured and a cord run through. This lamp, however, is fairly uncommon, and despite the fact that its physical integrity has been violated, it is still of interest to collectors who want an example of Gorham's mixed metalwork in a hard-to-find form.

What is it worth?

This lamp base sold at auction in 2004 for $1,645.

Item 34
Tiffany Mixed Metals Bowl

What is it? Tiffany and Company had been purchasing Japanese products to be sold in their store since around 1869, and examples of Japanese art were prominently displayed in various international exhibitions since 1862. Like Gorham, there were books on Japanese art in the Tiffany library, and Tiffany's principal silver designer, Edward C. Moore, was very familiar with Japanese taste and design from all these sources.

Tiffany made its first piece of Japanese-style silver around 1871, and it is thought that, initially, the company was influenced more by Western interpretation of Japanese themes done by other companies such as Christofle in France than by Japanese originals themselves. But the company was very interested in Japanese art, and they had Dr. Christopher Dresser (an English designer and tastemaker) collect about 2,000 pieces for them, many of which they sold at auction in 1877.

They retained some of the objects, however, and Moore began basing his designs on original Japanese metalwork. Tiffany made

Valued at $11,750

Footed ovoid bowl, 5 1/2 inches high and 7 3/4 inches diameter. The sterling silver body is hand hammered and has a rim on both the base and bowl with applied wave edge decoration. The exterior surface has been incised with stylized water ripples, and a silver frog rests on a copper lily pad along with a bee and a pair of carp. The base has another pair of carp: one brass, the other silver. The base is marked "Tiffany & Co. 6919 Makers 3855, Sterling Silver, 925-1000 M."

Japanese-influenced metalwares using a number of decorative techniques, including engraving, chasing, and applying areas of mixed metalwork to add color and texture to the surface.

To increase the visual interest in the surface of the metal, the pieces customarily were hand hammered, and oxidation was added to heighten the drama of the play of light across the contrasting light and dark areas. This is why great care needs to be taken when cleaning mixed metalwares because damaging or lessening these effects can greatly affect both the aesthetic and monetary value of the items.

The bowl pictured here was made using copper, brass, and silver applied to the surface of the hammered silver bowl to give it an aquatic look executed in the Japanese manner. The marks on this piece indicate that it was made after 1875, and is probably circa 1885 (i.e., 1885 plus or minus ten years). The numbers beside the mark are the pattern number (6919) and the order number (3855).

What is it worth? This piece, which weighs approximately 20 troy ounces, sold at auction in July 2005 for $11,750.

Item 35
Saint Gaudens Bust

Valued at $127,000

Classical head mounted on a green marble base. The head is that of a woman wearing a crown of leaves. It is bronze with a brown/green patina and is 8 1/4 inches tall. It is signed and dated "A. Saint Gaudens M.C.M." and inscribed "Copyright MCMVII by Augustus Saint Gaudens." The condition is good.

What is it?

Most of the bronze statuary found in the United States is of European origin. This piece, however, is American and is the work of the important American artist Augustus Saint Gaudens. Saint Gaudens is perhaps best known to the collecting public for his striking design for the United States Indian-head ten-dollar gold piece or "Eagle" (minted 1907–33), and the standing Liberty twenty-dollar gold piece or "Double Eagle" (minted 1907–33).

Saint Gaudens was born in Dublin, Ireland, in 1848, but his family took their infant son to New York City when he was only six months old. Saint Gaudens finished school at thirteen and was apprenticed to a cameo maker, but he also took art classes at the Cooper Union and the National Academy of Design.

Saint Gaudens finished his apprenticeship at age nineteen and traveled to France, where he continued his art education under François Jouffry at the Ecole des Beaux-Arts. He left Paris for Rome, where he lived for five years while studying classical art, and there he married Augusta Horner.

His first major commission was for a statue of Admiral David Farragut, which was unveiled in New York City's Madison Square in 1876. After the success of this commission, Saint Gaudens's career took off, and he taught art at New York's Art Students League and established a studio with a large number of assistants.

In 1875, Saint Gaudens took commissions to design two magnificent pieces of silver for Tiffany & Company. One was a pair of 3-foot-tall candelabra that were made for James G. Bennett as sailing trophies. Saint Gaudens took inspiration for these from George Catlin's images of Native Americans. These pieces were sold at auction in 1886 for $3,500 (a princely sum at the time), and they have not been seen since.

The other commission Saint Gaudens accepted from Tiffany and Company involved a sterling silver vase made for the poet William Cullen Bryant. The vase itself was designed by Tiffany's James H. Whitehouse, but Saint Gaudens provided five of the medallions used to decorate the vase including one that featured a portrait of Bryant and others that showed scenes from the poet's life.

The head pictured above began as a study for the head of a figure of "Victory" (Nikh-Eiphnh), that was to be part of the General William Tecumseh Sherman monument that stands in New York's Grand Army Plaza just outside Central Park. The monument depicts the Civil War general on horseback being led by a striding allegorical figure of "Victory."

Saint Gaudens reportedly had a hard time achieving the look he wanted for the head of "Victory." The first attempt did not please him, so he began refining the head and using "beautiful features"—but he was not satisfied with this either, because he said it had too much "personality."

He returned to his first version for the Sherman monument, but continued to rework the second version over the years, and this piece is the result of that process. The 1907 (MCMVII) copyright date seen on this piece is also the year of the artist's death from cancer.

What is it worth? This piece sold at auction in May 2005 for $127,000.

Item 36

Bradley and Hubbard Bookend

Valued at $192.50

One-piece cast bronze image of
a bouquet of flowers in a shallow
neoclassical urn with a base. The
piece is 6 1/4 inches tall and is
signed "B & H." The paint is original
and in excellent condition.

What is it?

This piece looks a great deal like a doorstop, but it is not. Instead it is a bookend, and the "B & H" signature found on its reverse side indicates that it was made by the Bradley and Hubbard Company of Meriden, Connecticut. This prolific and prestigious company was founded in 1854 by Nathaniel L. Bradley and Walter Hubbard.

Until 1850, Bradley was a farmer but he abandoned the soil and began selling clocks instead. He was very successful, and in 1852 joined with the Hatch brothers to found the Bradley, Hatch Clock Company. This too was successful; but by 1854, the company needed money to expand. At this time, the Hatch brothers left the company and William L. Bradley and Walter Hubbard joined the enterprise to form Bradley and Hubbard.

The company was almost destroyed by the Civil War. Clocks were not selling, so they turned to making large quantities of flags. After the war, the kerosene lamp business was booming, and Bradley and Hubbard started making all kinds of lamps, lamp parts, chandeliers, and fixtures.

Bradley and Hubbard used brass, bronze, and iron to make their wares, and collectors find their initials on a great number of items other than lamps. These include desk sets, andirons, card receivers, chess tables, call bells (such as those used in hotels at the time), vases, umbrella stands, frames, pipe trays, candlesticks, plant stands, and bookends.

Bradley and Hubbard was known for the quality of their casting work and the intricacy of their designs, which tended to reflect the latest fashions of the time in which they were made. In 1940, Bradley and Hubbard was purchased by the Charles Parker Company, which was part of the Union Manufacturing Company.

It is unfortunate that this is a single bookend, because just as with candlesticks, collectors prefer their bookends to be in pairs. However, this one, which dates from the first quarter of the 20th century, is attractive enough to stand on its own. It should be noted that doorstops that look very similar to this were made, but the doorstops, about 2 inches taller, were generally made from iron and are somewhat heavier.

What is it worth?

The value of this particular single bookend is enhanced by the superb condition of its original paint. This bookend sold at auction in May 2005 for $192.50. If there had been a pair, this price might have tripled.

Item 37
"Goddess of Liberty" Weathervane

Valued at $380,000

Figure of a woman in a cap holding a flagpole with a thirty-two-star American flag. The piece is made from copper and the figure is 15 1/2 inches tall; total height including the flag pole is 19 3/4 inches. The piece has old red, white, and blue paint, and is resting on a contemporary oval base fitted for a rod to secure the flagpole.

What is it? This weathervane is a representation of the Goddess of Liberty, and she is wearing a traditional liberty cap, with a laurel wreath, and a bandolier running diagonally from shoulder to waist. It is somewhat similar to another Goddess of Liberty weathervane that carried the label of J. W. Fiske Ironworks (also known as J. W. Fiske Architectural Metals) of New York City and Paterson, New Jersey.

A weathervane can be in almost any shape as long as it has a body to catch the breezes, a pointer to indicate direction, and a spindle on which it can turn freely. The first weathervane in recorded history was the one atop the Tower of the Winds in Athens, Greece. Built in 48 B.C. by the astronomer Andronicus, the tower's weathervane was a representation of the god Triton with the body of a man and the tail of a fish.

In the ancient world, weathervanes often had the bodies of gods such as Aeolus (god of wind), Boreas (the north wind), and Hermes or Mercury (god of all sorts of things, including commerce and gambling). In later years, the Vikings used weathervanes on their ships, and in the 9th century A.D., the pope decreed that every church in Christendom had to have a weathervane in the shape of a rooster—thus the alternative for weathervanes, "weather cocks."

The first recorded weathervane maker in the American colonies was Deacon Shem Drowne, who was responsible for making the most famous weathervane: the grasshopper atop Boston's Faneuil Hall. In the United States, the most commonly seen weathervane style is of an American eagle followed by a horse. After that, weathervanes come in almost every style imaginable including Native Americans, railroad trains, dirigibles, airplanes, automobiles, men in sulkies, firemen on fire engines and fire wagons, and farmyard animals such as pigs, rams, and cows; other animals such as deer, dogs, pigeons, squirrels, fish, storks, goats, and peacocks; and inanimate objects such as plows and even a representation of a cut nail.

Weathervanes are said to come in two varieties: the ones that are handmade by individuals and those that are factory made by famous makers such as L. W. Cushing, A. L. Jewel & Company, E. G. Washburn and Company, Harris and Company, and J. W. Fiske. This last concern was founded by Joseph Winn Fiske in New York City in 1858, and primarily made architectural metalware. The company moved to Paterson, New Jersey in the 1950s and was in business until 1982.

When the company closed, the molds for making the weather-vanes were sent to the American Folk Art Museum, which in turn passed them along to the New York State Museum in Albany. Most of the molds still in existence are of horses, but there are also examples of molds to make three different cows, a running deer, four different eagles, a bull, a crowing rooster, and others.

Missing are the Fiske molds for a variety of other vanes including all three versions of the ox, the swan, the greyhound, all three sizes of the elephant, the dragon, the ocean steamer, the ferry-boat, and the Goddess of Liberty. That weathervane can be seen on page 24 of J. W. Fiske's 1875 catalog, where it was priced for a not inconsiderable $25.

The example of the Goddess of Liberty pictured above is similar to one with a Fiske label that was sold by Northeast Auctions for $424,000. The piece sold by Northeast is the same size as the one shown here, but there are some variations, and an absolute attribution to J. W. Fiske is not possible.

What is it worth? This fine weathervane from the fourth quarter of the 19th century sold at auction in August 2005 for $380,000.

Item 38
A. L. Jewel "Centaur" Weathervane

What is it? In an advertisement that appeared around 1864, the A. L. Jewel Company of Waltham, Massachusetts, claimed to be the manufacturers of "78 varieties of Copper Weather Vanes." The ad went on to say that they made images of "Horses, Cattle, Sheep, Eagle (sic), Church Vanes, Arrows, Scrolls, &c." In addition, the company made "All kinds of vanes Made to Order." Interestingly, that advertisement was decorated with a representation of the Goddess of Columbia, which is very similar to the Fiske Goddess of Liberty discussed in the previous section.

Alvin L. Jewell founded the A. L. Jewel Company in Waltham, Massachusetts, in 1852, but the company came to an untimely end in 1867. In that year, Jewel was putting up a sign on a building when the scaffolding he was standing on collapsed and he was killed.

Subsequently, Jewel's shop, tools, weathervane patterns, and molds were sold to the highest bidder, Josephus Harris of Brattleboro, Vermont. For some reason, Harris did not pay the $7,975 that he had bid for the property. At that point, Leonard W. Cushing and Stillman White of Waltham offered $7,950, and the assets of the A. L. Jewel Company became theirs.

Valued at $51,700

Weathervane depicting a centaur with drawn bow and arrow. The piece is made from molded copper and cast lead and is 32 1/4 inches high by 39 1/4 inches wide. The molded body is flattened and has a sheet copper tail. The surface is covered with verdigris, and there are vestiges of yellow sizing, gilt, and black paint. There are some repairs.

Cushing and White began selling "The Celebrated Waltham Copper Weather Vanes" using Jewel's molds, but over the years, they added new designs of their own. In 1872, Cushing bought White's interest and the company became L. W. Cushing and Sons, which was reportedly in existence until 1932. In 1883, Cushing advertised that his business had been in operation since 1852, which clearly indicates that he thought of himself as the successor to Jewel.

Sometimes, Jewel weathervanes are found signed "A. L. Jewel & Co. Waltham, Mass." on the side, but this one is not marked. The circa 1860 weathervane pictured here is attributed to Jewell because it is similar to one of his in the collection of the Shelburne Museum in Shelburne, Vermont, and because at least one authoritative reference on the subject credits Jewel with this particular design.

What is it worth?
The centaur weathervane sold at auction in June 2005 for $51,700.

Item 39
Gamecock Weathervane

Valued at $11,750

Weathervane in the form of a gamecock. It has a flattened full body made from molded copper and a sheet copper tail. There is a great deal of detailing on the body of the bird, which stands on an arrow with an iron tip and corrugated sheet copper feathering. The copper has been gilded and the surface has been worn by significant exposure to weather. The figure without the stand is 21 1/2 inches tall by 25 3/4 inches long. There are no repairs.

What is it? The two weathervanes previously discussed can each be attributed to a specific maker, but this one cannot. There is no doubt that it is American and from the 19th century, but this piece has no provenance and cannot be assigned to a particular maker.

Looking at a copper weathervane such as this one it might be difficult to understand how it was made, and how involved its manufacture really was. It is said that even the simplest hollow, "swell body" or "full body" weathervane required more than a dozen molds to produce the final form. A vane with a "swell body" is one that has the figure puffed out or "swollen" but is still somewhat flat. A vane with a "full body" is just that; it is fully developed and looks like a three-dimensional model of the thing that is being represented.

Each of these hollow type weathervanes started with a pattern that was then turned into a three-dimensional wooden model by a carver. The manufacturer then took this model, cut it in half, and then cut up the various sections such as head, body, tail, talons, or whatever form the figure might have.

The next step was to have molds made of these various sections. Then, a coppersmith hammered sheet copper into the mold until it took on the proper shape, and finally the whole thing was assembled. A ball might be added for the figure to stand or perch on, and this required yet more molds. Lastly, the letters of the cardinal directions (north, east, south, and west) had to be added and a stand constructed. It was a very labor-intensive process.

What is it worth? This gamecock weathervane sold at auction in August 2004 for $11,750.

Item40
Daguerreotype of Millard Fillmore

$10,281

Photographic image on a copper plate of a distinguished-looking gentleman. The surface has a silvery sheen and is in a leather case partially lined with velvet that measures 3 5/8 by 3 1/8 inches. The picture itself is surrounded by an oval brass cut-out mat and gilded brass preserver frame.

What is it?

What is it? The first permanent photograph was produced on a pewter plate in 1827 using a device called a "camera obscura," which is a lightproof box with a convex lens at one end and a screen at the other on which images could be projected. This device had been used since the 16th century to capture likenesses and scenes that were then traced or drawn by artists.

The person who used the camera obscura to make the first permanent photograph was Frenchman Joseph-Nicephore Niepce. In 1829, he went into partnership with Louis Jacques Mande Daguerre, an artist in Paris. Unfortunately, Niepce died in 1833, and the perfection of the first commercially viable photographic process was left to Daguerre.

Daguerre introduced his process for capturing images on a copper plate on January 7, 1839, in Paris. The French government was so impressed that they gave Daguerre a pension for life in exchange for the secrets to his process, which they then published as a gift to the world. Daguerre's images were called Daguerreotypes, and they were immensely popular until the 1850s, when they were supplanted by images on glass (called "ambrotype"), images on tin (called "ferrotypes" or "tintypes"), and images on paper (called a variety of things, including "Calotypes," and "Talbotypes").

Daguerreotypes are distinguished by the relatively thick copper plate they are on, and by their silvery, almost mirrorlike surface. Daguerreotypes came in a variety of sizes with the 1/16 plate measuring 1 3/8 by 1 5/8 inches, the 1/9 plate measuring 2 by 2 1/2 inches, the 1/8 plate measuring 2 1/8 by 3 3/4 inches, the 1/6 plate measuring 2 5/8 by 3 1/4 inches, the 1/4 plate measuring 3 1/8 by 4 1/8 inches, the half plate measuring 4 1/2 by 5 1/2 inches, and the full plate measuring 6 1/2 by 8 1/2 inches.

Larger-format daguerreotypes are rarer than the smaller-sized examples, and the piece pictured above is a 1/6 plate, which is a commonly found size. These plates were made by plating a thin layer of silver on top of a much thicker layer of copper and then giving this an acid wash to remove impurities. Next, the plate was placed in a box and exposed to iodine vapors to sensitize it to light. When the plate was put into a camera that had been designed by Daguerre, and the shutter opened to let in ambient light, the image of whatever was in front of the lens was captured on the light-sensitive plate's copper and silver surface.

This exposure could last for anywhere from five to thirty minutes, and required the sitter to be absolutely still during this period. It must have been very difficult to take a picture of a child or a fidgety person. Animals were nearly impossible to capture, and landscapes were difficult because the wind blew trees, animals entered the shot, and things were always moving.

The daguerreotype came to the United States very quickly. The inventor Samuel F. B. Morse visited Daguerre in his Parisian studio early in 1839 and took the process back with him in September of that same year. Soon daguerreotype studios were popping up all over America, and it became the vogue to have your picture taken instead of being captured in much more expensive oil paint.

In 1844, Mathew Brady received instruction in the Daguerre process from Morse and opened a gallery across the street from P. T. Barnum's museum in New York City. Brady got the idea of recording the visage of important personages of the day, which he called his "Gallery of Illustrious Americans." Brady photographed every American president from John Quincy Adams to William McKinley—with the exception of William Henry Harrison, who died three years before Brady began his work as a photographer. If not for Brady's work, the image of many political figures of the early to mid-19th century would not have come down to us.

The daguerreotype pictured here is of a famous American, but it was not taken by Mathew Brady. Its maker is anonymous, but the portrait is of the 13th president of the United States, Millard Fillmore (1800–74). Fillmore was never elected to the presidency, but was Zachary Taylor's vice president and served from July 1850 to March 1853 after Taylor's untimely death.

Daguerreotype portraits of notable Americans and politicians are highly desired by collectors. They will pay large sums for good examples in excellent condition. This particular portrait of Fillmore is similar to one in the National Portrait Gallery of the Smithsonian Institution, which was taken in the studio of Albert Sands Southworth and Josiah Johnson Hawkes in Boston. This pair worked together from 1844 to 1861.

What is it worth? This circa 1850 daguerreotype of Millard Fillmore sold at auction in June 2005 for $10,281.

Related item

Photographic image on a copper plate with a brass cutout mat surrounded by a gilded brass frame. The image itself is covered with a sheet of glass and held in a leather case with embossed designs in the rococo manner. The piece is 3 5/8 by 3 1/8 inches.

What is it?

It is estimated that over the run of their popularity, more than 30 million daguerreotypes were made in the United States and millions more were made overseas. Most are portraits of people whose identity like this one has been lost over time.

Every major city in the United States had a portrait studio specializing in making daguerreotype portraits for a few dollars each. As has been said, exposure times were lengthy. When an attempt was made to photograph children, the little ones might actually be tied to the chair on which they sat with a sash that looked like part of their clothing in the finished picture.

Most photographers' chairs had a U-shaped device called a head rest that was designed to hold the head motionless while the camera was working its magic. When the process was set to begin, the photographer took a freshly polished and mercury vapor–sensitized copper plate and slipped it into the camera. A slide covered the plate to protect it from the light, and when that was removed, the lens cap was removed and the exposure begun.

During the protracted exposure time, the camera operators sometimes recited specific poems, not so much to amuse and distract the sitter but to measure the time. After the exposure was completed, the plate was taken to a darkened room, where it was put in a mercury fuming box and developed. The image was then made permanent in a fixing solution composed of hyposulfate of soda. Next, the plate was immersed in gold chloride to tone the image and protect it.

After that, any tinting that was to be done was added using powdered pigments. In the United States, a brass mat was then added on top of the finished daguerreotype and a piece of glass placed over this three-layer sandwich. Finally, the picture was placed in a case that was made from materials such as leather or papier-mâché.

What is it worth?

Daguerreotypes such as this one are not hard to find. Families often have drawers full of them, and unless the subject is special in some way, the monetary value can be very modest. The insurance replacement value is $100.

BRASS

Item 41
Philadelphia Andirons

Valued at $28,200

Pair of brass and iron andirons 28 inches tall with urn tops on columnar shafts and minor wear. The urns have ball finials and engraved guilloche borders with foliate and swag decoration. The columns themselves are encircled by engraved bellflower vines and have cubic plinths engraved with a sunburst and an eagle with a shield with stars motif. There are spurred cabriole legs that terminate in ball-and-claw feet.

What is it? Andirons made in the United States in the 18th century typically have four kinds of feet. "Penny" feet have had the ends of their legs hammered flat into a disk so that they look something like a penny coin. There are those that have feet that have a bulbous shape that resembles a hoe and these are called "slipper feet."

There are those that have feet that are shaped like balls (these were popular well into the 19th century), and there are those which have legs that terminate in a claw clutching a ball. In furniture this kind of foot is associated with both Queen Anne and Chippendale furniture as well as what the British refer to as Georgian furniture. For andirons, ball-and-claw feet were popular during the late third quarter and throughout the entire fourth quarter of the 18th century.

Columnar andirons like the ones pictured here with their urn finials and square plinths are often associated with Philadelphia, and a number of different types of engravings are found on the plinths. One that is often connected to the commemoration of the death of George Washington in 1799 featured the image of a willow tree with an urn.

Others had an anchor with a chain with a starburst placed within a border of repeating triangular figures. Examples with this motif often had a design on the other faces that resembled a compass. This imagery was supposedly a reference to the state arms of Rhode Island and was popular in the years leading up to the War of 1812.

The Federal-inspired motifs on the pair of andirons pictured here are a bit more crudely engraved than some, but the eagle with shield image is very desirable to collectors of Americana. This pair is from the late 18th century.

What is it worth? This particular pair of American Federal ball-and-claw-footed andirons sold at auction in February 2005 for $28,200.

Item 42
R. Wittingham Andirons

Valued at $9,000

Pair of brass-and-iron andirons with spire and urn finials above faceted shafts with similar finials on the log stops behind. The shaft and the log stop are separated by a pierced gallery, and the arched spurred legs terminate in ball feet. The pair is 23 inches tall and signed "R. Wittingham, N York."

What is it? Richard Wittingham was a brazier in New York City who reportedly worked from 1795 to 1818, although one source says that his son Richard Wittingham Jr. took over the business in 1813. Unlike most American brass makers, Wittingham signed some—but not all—of his work and is known for his fine andirons, particularly those with spire and urn finials with pierced galleries between the front shaft and the log stop.

This very elegant detail can be found in at least two patterns, the one shown here and one that has the image of an eagle among scrolling tendrils. Of these two, the gallery with the eagle is of much more interest to modern collectors than the plainer version that does not have the patriotic overtones.

Other andirons made in New York City during the first quarter of the 19th century can be found marked by various other makers including Bailey, O. Phillips, and the partnership of Griffiths and Green.

What is it worth? This pair of Richard Wittingham–signed andirons sold at auction in August 2005 for $9,000.

Item 43
Skimmer

Valued at $600

Skimmer with pierced brass bowl and wrought-iron handle. The brass bowl is rounded and attached with copper rivets in three places to a wrought-iron handle with a crook at the end. It is signed "I. Whitman," and the length is 20 inches.

What is it? Kitchen tools of every variety and almost every age have a fascination for modern collectors. Fairly modern examples with painted wooden handles are of interest, but serious collectors are particularly interested in those examples from the 19th century or earlier that are handmade and have wrought-iron handles made by blacksmiths.

Skimmers are simple tools, usually consisting of a long handle with some sort of perforated shallow bowl at the end. They were used to skim solids or semisolids from other liquids, especially the greasy froth that forms on soups and stews as they boil. Skimmers also could be used to remove fried foods from a kettle, and to skim molasses, maple sugar, or, more commonly, milk. These were very useful utensils, and no kitchen of the 19th century was complete without a good skimmer.

This piece was made in two parts—the shallow brass bowl and the blacksmith-made wrought-iron handle. The handle is signed "I. Whitman," which is probably for J. Whitman, who worked in

Reading, Pennsylvania, from about 1800 to 1830. Other brass and wrought-iron items are associated with Whitman, and it is thought that he may have been responsible just for crafting the handle—although he may have done both parts and riveted the two together.

What is it worth? This skimmer sold at auction in August 2005 for $600.

Item 44
Candlesticks

Valued at $1,500

Pair of brass candlesticks, 9 3/4 inches tall. They have a stepped domed base that is attached to the shaft with a threaded protrusion made from the end of the brass column. The column has a faceted knop below the faceted octagonal shaft that rises to another somewhat flattened knop and terminates in an octagonal candle cup with molded rim. The inside of the base is very smooth, and the candlesticks have a great deal of surface patina.

What is it? Through advertisements in period newspapers, it is known that American brass founders made candlesticks, candelabra, and other lighting devices—but no signed examples have ever been found. This creates a problem of attribution, because American brass tends to be very similar to the brass that was being made in England at the same time. In other words, there is no sure way to determine whether or not a given pair of candlesticks is American or English.

The pair pictured here has been attributed to this side of the Atlantic because they are similar to a pair to which Colonial Williamsburg has assigned an American origin, but this may or may not be correct. What can be said with some certainty is that this pair is from the early 18th century.

Candlesticks made during this time period can be identified generally by the manner in which they were constructed—and this technique was the same on both sides of the Atlantic. For the most part, the columns of the candlesticks of this era (from the early to mid-18th century) were cast in halves and then soldered together with a solder that was the color of brass. When done properly (as it usually was), this join between the two halves virtually disappears and can be very hard to detect even with a close, thorough examination.

This method of "casting halves" allowed the shafts to be somewhat hollow, which saved on metal and made for lighter weight candlesticks. The base was cast as a separate piece. After it had been filed and burnished, the end of the candlestick's column was threaded so that it could be screwed into the base.

This provides a good clue to the age because the threads will be obviously hand cut, coarse, and somewhat uneven. They will not have the evenness of a machine-cut screw, and it should be evident that they were not made using a modern tap and die set. The base itself furnishes another clue to age; it will be well finished and smooth, while the majority of the later reproductions have a base that is relatively rough and unfinished.

The age of this particular pair is determined by all the factors mentioned above and by the characteristic shape of the candle cup, domed base, and shaft.

What is it worth? Pairs of authentic 18th-century candlesticks such as this one have become increasingly difficult to find, and the insurance replacement value of this pair is $1,500.

COIN
SILVER

Item 45
Samuel Edwards Butter Plate

What is it? Pre–Revolutionary War American silver is highly prized by collectors, and prices can be considerable for examples by famous silversmiths or items that have an impeccable provenance. The coin-silver butter plate shown here was made by Samuel Edwards, a member of a highly regarded family of Boston silversmiths, and the plate is one of a documented pair with the other now in the Boston Museum of Fine Arts.

John Edwards, Samuel's father, was born in England in 1671, and is believed to have come to Boston with his family in 1685. It is speculated that Edwards apprenticed under the highly regarded Boston silversmith, Jeremiah Dummer, because of a beaker in South Carolina that closely resembles Dummer's work. Edwards married the granddaughter of Governor John Winthrop and established himself as one of Boston's finest craftsmen.

Valued at $38,775

Silver-colored metal butter plate, 5 15/16 inches in diameter and 4 troy ounces. The plate has a broad rim that is engraved with a coat of arms in a sheaf of grain and scroll cartouche plus another crest opposite. The bottom of the plate is flat and has an indented center point. In script on the underside is "E. Jackson," and nearer the center point are the initials "S E" contained in a shaped cartouche with a star below and a stylized crown above.

John Edwards was married twice, and Samuel (1705–62) was the son of his first wife. Samuel's brother, Thomas, was also a silversmith, and both probably apprenticed under their father. Thomas died less than ten years after his father, and his recorded pieces are far fewer in number than those made by either his father or his brother.

One of the marks used by Samuel Edwards

This plate first appeared as one of a pair in a 1757 list made of Edward Jackson's inventory. One of the pair was given to the Museum of Fine Arts, Boston in the 1950s by the family of Guy Lovell. Lovell was the designer of the current museum facility.

What is it worth? This small plate with the big history and famous maker sold at auction in 2005 for $38,775!

What is it? The spoons pictured here are the sort of coin-silver items that turn up with some regularity. Many homes across the United States have similar spoons, and one of the more interesting things about them is that they can provide insight into family history.

As was said earlier, home owners often took excess coins to the local silversmith to have them turned into useful items, and in many if not most cases, the owners had the pieces monogrammed to help establish them as their personal property. Their descendants can look at these monograms and figure out (or try to figure out) to which of their ancestors the monogram belonged. Then

Valued at **$965**

Collection of six spoons made from silver-colored metal. There are four teaspoons: one marked "Hope" with Masonic symbols, another marked "CAB," the third is marked "W. Homes," and the fourth is marked "F R" with a dot between the two initials. In addition, there are two tablespoons, one is marked "Duhme," and the other is marked "Dumoutet." Three of the teaspoons are 6 inches long; the fourth is 5 3/4 inches. One tablespoon is 8 inches long, and the other is 9 1/4 inches long.

they can look at the mark and consult the lists of American silversmiths to identify the maker of the spoon, where he or she worked, and when. This information can help establish where and when a particular ancestor lived in the distant past and can supply a vital clue that might help establish a family's genealogy.

Sometimes all that collectors can find of a given silversmith's work are teaspoons and tablespoons—and perhaps a small ladle. On occasion, a mug or some sort of other small drinking vessel such as a julep cup will turn up, but large, elaborately embellished, decorative pieces are quite rare.

One of the marks used
by Thomas Hope

Mark used by
Charles Burnett

Mark used by
William Homes

Mark used by
John Baptiste Dumoutet

As for the spoons shown here, the teaspoon signed "Hope" was made by David Large Hope, who worked in Knoxville, Tennessee from about 1828 until his death in 1869. Hope was made a Master Mason in 1828, and his pieces are often marked with one or Masonic symbols that include a caliper. It is speculated that he had his own shop until about 1852, and the teaspoon shown here is from about 1850.

It should be noted that David Large Hope is not well known outside of the area in which he worked. In fact, many of the standard reference books on the subject of American silver do not mention his name, and the information that is available can be found only in a book on Tennessee silver by Dr. Benjamin Hubbard Caldwell Jr. and perhaps in other references with a focus on Southern silver. Collectors need to keep in mind that this is not an isolated instance; many regional silversmiths are either overlooked or misidentified, and much basic research still needs to be done.

The teaspoon signed "CAB" was made by Charles A. Burnett, who began his silversmith career in Alexandria, Virginia, in the late 18th century, but moved to Georgetown, District of Columbia, around 1800. Burnett signed some of his pieces just with his initials, but others he signed "C A Burnett" in a rectangular punch with raised dots between the "C," the "A," and the "B." This latter mark was sometimes accompanied by a representation of an eagle's head.

It is said that Burnett was the leading silversmith in our nation's capital during the Federal era, and he made pieces for presidents as well as for the Office of Indian Trade. Burnett's silver can be found in the Smithsonian Institution, the National Museum of the American Indian, and the Department of State. The teaspoon shown here is probably from the first quarter of the 19th century.

The third teaspoon was made by William Homes, who worked in Boston, Massachusetts, between 1739 and 1780. He signed his pieces in a number of ways, including just his initials "W H," only his last name "Homes," or "W Homes." Homes has two pieces in the Boston Museum of Fine Arts (a punch bowl and a porringer) and is a highly regarded craftsman. The spoon pictured is monogrammed "PH" within an oval reserve and is circa 1770.

The last teaspoon, which is marked "F R" in a rectangular punch, was made by Francis Richardson II (or Jr., 1705–82), a member of the second generation of the Richardson family of silversmiths who worked in Philadelphia. This dynasty was founded by Francis Richardson I (1681–1729), who used the initials "F R" in a heart-shaped punch.

Francis or "Frank" Richardson Jr. trained to be a silversmith under the tutelage of his father, but the younger Richardson also became a merchant as well as a maker and repairer of clocks. By the mid-1740s, it is thought that Francis Jr. had turned his attention more to being a merchant and made little silver after this point. Joseph Richardson, Francis Jr.'s brother, is thought to be the most accomplished of all the silversmiths in the Richardson family, and his work is most desired by collectors.

The first tablespoon, marked "Duhme," was made in Cincinnati, Ohio, by Duhme and Company, a jewelry company with manufacturing facilities. This company was founded by Herman Duhme in the early 1840s and was in business until 1907. Over the years, this firm made all kinds of metal items including coin silver, silver plate, and later, sterling silver.

The other tablespoon was made by John Baptiste Dumoutet. The last name was spelled several different ways including Doumoutet, Dymotit, Dumontot, and Dumorte. He began his career as a silversmith in Philadelphia in the late 18th century, but moved to Charleston, South Carolina, around 1802, where he continued working until about 1813. The teaspoon pictured here was made circa 1810 in Charleston.

What is it worth? Most coin-silver teaspoons are worth only a modest amount of money and can be purchased from retail sources sometimes for less than $20 each and, in most cases, the insurance replacement value does not exceed $50. Tablespoons are somewhat harder to find, but their value is generally less than $100.

It should be noted that monograms on sterling silver cause significant deductions, but monograms on American coin silver do not, and most collectors view these initials as decoration.

■ The David Large Hope teaspoon: Hope is largely unknown outside of his home state of Tennessee, and if one of his spoons were to turn up in the West or Northeast, it might go unappreciated and largely unrecognized because so few references mention him. In fact, this particular teaspoon was purchased in 2004 at a retail source in Denver for just $6. In his home area, this David Hope teaspoon is worth $175.

■ The Charles A. Burnett teaspoon: Burnett is an important American silversmith of the Federal period, and examples of his work can be found in both Mt. Vernon and Monticello. Collectors are very interested in Burnette's work, and a single spoon is valued at $150. Burnette's spoons are far more valuable when found in multiples and sets.

■ The William Homes teaspoon: Although Homes is an important Boston-area silversmith, a single teaspoon of his is valued at $40, while a set of four is commonly priced at $250. It is easy to assume that if one teaspoon is worth $40, the value for a set of four is just a matter of simple multiplication, and that the four would be worth $160. This, however, is not the case, because collectors prefer multiples over single pieces, and sets or multiples are much harder to find.

■ The Francis Richardson II teaspoon: The work of this Philadelphia silversmith is highly desired, and this tablespoon's value is $100.

■ The Duhme tablespoon: The work by this silversmith and jewelry company owner is most prized in Ohio, particularly in the Cincinnati area. Outside Cincinnati, it is valued at $50, but that price doubles in the vicinity of where it was made.

■ The Dumoutet tablespoon: Examples of silver made by smiths in major Southern cities such as Charleston and New Orleans before the Civil War are highly prized by collectors. The price depends to a certain degree on how readable the marks are, and the ones on this example are clear and easily discerned. It should be valued at $400.

Item 47
Paul Revere Tablespoon

Valued at $9,000

Tablespoon engraved with the
initials "JSD" engraved in script at
the top of the handle. This spoon
is 8 3/4 inches long and has a
down-turned rounded-end handle
with oval bowl and molded
drop. On the back the
piece is marked "Revere"
in a rectangular punch
that has an uneven lower
line. The piece weighs 2
troy ounces.

What is it?

The question above—"What is it?"—may seem simple in this case, but it is not. There were actually three American silversmiths named Paul Revere, and the important question is which one of these three made this particular spoon.

One of the marks used by Paul (Apollos) Revere, Sr.

The story of this spoon really starts in Riancaud (or Reocaud), France, in 1702 when Apollos Rivoire was born to a Huguenot family. At the tender age of thirteen he was sent to America to avoid religious persecution and to start a new life in a new world. Rivoire arrived in Boston in 1716 and became apprenticed to silversmith John Coney (1655–1722).

One of the marks used by Paul (Apollos) Revere, Sr.

When Coney died, Rivoire established his own business in Dock Square in Boston, and in the 1720s began the process of anglicizing his name to Paul Revere. In 1729, Revere married Deborah Hitchourn (also spelled Hichborn or Hitchborn), and they had between nine and twelve children, depending on the source consulted. However, there is no disagreement that only seven survived and that of these, the eldest son was given his father's new anglicized name and is known to history as Paul Revere II or Paul Revere Jr.

Sampling of marks used by Paul Revere, Jr., the patriot

No one seems to know exactly when the younger Paul Revere was born. The records of Boston's New Brick Congregational Church list his baptism as being on December 22, 1734, but that was according to the Julian calendar, which was in use throughout the British Empire until 1752. According to the Gregorian calendar, which we all now use, the date of the baptism was January 2, 1735, and this means that the man who became known for his famous ride from Charleston to Lexington was probably born sometime in late December 1734.

Young Paul Revere II received his early education at Boston's North Writing School, but he was apprenticed later to his father to learn how to be a silversmith. The younger Paul Revere took over the family business after his father's death in 1754, but he volunteered to fight in the Lake George Campaign of the French and Indian War.

Paul Revere II married twice and had eight children by his first wife, who died in 1773, and then eight more children by his second wife, who died in 1813. Some speculate that the responsibility of supporting such a large family caused him to be involved in a lot of different businesses.

In addition to being a silversmith whose work was respected even in England, he was also an engraver of copper plates, a printer, and a dentist. He is known to have carved wooden false teeth and wired them into the mouths of patients. In addition, he opened a gunpowder mill during the Revolutionary War, and then after the war operated a hardware store, a foundry, and a copper rolling mill.

Paul Revere II's first son by his first wife was named Paul Revere, often referred to as Paul Revere Jr. or Paul Revere III. He was born in 1760 and followed his father and grandfather in becoming a silversmith, but he predeceased his father and died in 1813 (Paul II did not die until 1818).

Therefore, there were three Paul Reveres making silver in America during the 18th and early 19th century, and the marks of Apollos Rivoire and his son are fairly similar. The marks of Paul Revere II, the American patriot, are distinct in that they use letters that are somewhat different from those his father used.

There is no doubt that this spoon is by Paul Revere the patriot, and because of the "JSD" monogram, there is a possibility that it is one of the spoons Revere made for Jennie S. Dunbar of Scituate, Massachusetts.

What is it worth? In the discussion before this one we said that teaspoons and tablespoons are the most common forms of American colonial and coin silver found by collectors and that most of them are relatively inexpensive. The work of Paul Revere is an important exception, and because of Revere's historical importance, this example sold at auction in August 2005 for $9,000.

STERLING
SILVER

Item 48

Kirk Flatware, "Repousse"

Valued at $4,835; $8,134

Teaspoon, knife, and fork from a flatware set consisting of twelve each of 7 1/4-inch place forks; 6 1/4-inch salad forks; 4 3/8-inch demitasse spoons; 7 5/8-inch ice-tea spoons: 8 5/- inch place knives; 6 3/8-inch oval-bowl soup spoons; 5 1/4-inch individual butter spreaders; twenty-four 5 7/8-inch teaspoons; three 8 3/8-inch serving spoons; and one 6-inch sugar shell; one 8 1/2-inch cold-meat fork; one 10 1/4-inch pie server with silver plated blade; one 7-inch gravy ladle; and large ice tongs with claw end. The pieces are all marked "S. Kirk & Son, Inc," and are not monogrammed.

What is it?

Samuel Kirk was born in Doylestown, Pennsylvania, in 1793 to a family who had been in the silversmithing business in England since the 17th century. At age seventeen, Samuel was apprenticed to Philadelphia silversmith James Howell. After completing his training he moved to Baltimore, Maryland, and entered into a partnership with John Smith.

The coin-silver wares crafted by this partnership are found marked either "K & S" or "Kirk and Smith," with both accompanied by a set of marks from the Baltimore assay office. These generally consisted of three punch marks—a shield, a letter of the alphabet, and a head in profile (which may have been the head of George Washington used in place of the head of the British sovereign). Sometimes, only two punch marks were used and the head was omitted.

Smith left the business in 1820, and the firm became known as just Samuel Kirk. This continued until 1846, when Kirk's son Henry Child Kirk joined the firm and it became S. Kirk and Son. In 1861, this partnership was joined by two other Kirk children, Charles and Clarence, and the firm became known as S. Kirk and Sons. In 1868, these two younger sons left the firm and the name reverted to S. Kirk and Son.

Samuel Kirk died in 1872, and Henry Child Kirk continued in the business, still calling it S. Kirk and Son. His son Henry Child Kirk Jr. came into the business in 1890. Like all the children and grandchildren of Samuel Kirk who became partners in the business, he apprenticed in the trade and was a qualified silver craftsman.

In 1828, Samuel Kirk introduced a new style of decoration to America called repoussé. This involved hand-hammering a design from underneath so that a raised decoration appeared on the top surface of the silver. This decoration is often enhanced by chasing, which uses a hammer and punch to emboss decorations into the surface without the loss of metal. To many modern collectors, Kirk "Repousse" refers to a flatware pattern that has been made since 1828 and is still being made to this day by the same company, now known as the Kirk Stieff Company. Initially, this flatware was made in coin silver, and over the years, it has been produced in several variations. The pieces pictured to the left are all marked "S. Kirk & Son Inc.," which indicates they were made after about 1925 but before 1932.

S. KIRK & SON INC. STERLING

One of the marks used
by S. Kirk and Son.

What is it worth?

Since this pattern is still being made, we quote retail prices both on the secondary market (Replacements, Ltd.) and on the primary market—the suggested retail prices provided by Kirk Stieff. Prices are rounded off to the nearest dollar. This procedure will be used for all the other sterling silver flatware patterns which follow.

Replacements.com:

a.	Twelve 7 1/4-inch place forks @ $38 each	$ 456
b.	Twelve 6 1/4-inch salad forks @ $40 each	$ 480
c.	Twenty-four 5 7/8-inch teaspoons @ $23 each	$ 552
d.	Twelve 4 3/8-inch demitasse spoons @ $28 each	$ 336
e.	Twelve 7 5/8-inch ice-tea spoons @ $40 each	$ 480
f.	Twelve 8 5/8-inch place knives @ $55 each	$ 660
g.	Twelve 6 3/8-inch oval-bowl soup spoons @ $46 each	$ 552
h.	Twelve 5 1/2-inch butter spreaders (hollow handles) @ $37 each	$ 444
i.	Three 8 3/8-inch serving spoons @ $60 each	$ 180
j.	One 6-inch sugar shell @ $30	$ 30
k.	One 8 1/2-inch cold-meat fork @ $100	$ 100
l.	One 10 1/4-inch pie server with silver plated blade @ $90	$ 90
m.	One 7-inch gravy ladle @ $75	$ 75
n.	One pair of large ice tongs with claw end @ $400	$ 400
		TOTAL SET $ 4,835

Kirk Stieff suggested retail prices:

a.	Twelve place forks @ $69 each	$ 828
b.	Twelve salad forks @ $68 each	$ 816
c.	Twenty-four teaspoons @ $68 each	$ 1,632
d.	Twelve demitasse spoons @ $66 each	$ 792
e.	Twelve ice-tea spoons @ $68 each	$ 816
f.	Twelve place knives @ $66 each	$ 792
g.	Twelve oval-bowl soup spoons @ $68 each	$ 816
h.	Twelve butter spreaders (hollow handles) @ $66 each	$ 792
i.	Three serving spoons @ $138 each	$ 414
j.	One sugar shell @ $138	$ 138
k.	One medium cold-meat fork @ $104	$ 104
l.	One pie and cake server @ $56	$ 56
m.	One gravy ladle @ $138	$ 138
		TOTAL SET $ 8,134

Related item

Tea set consisting of a teapot, a coffeepot, a cream pitcher, a covered sugar bowl, and a waste bowl. Four of the pieces have rounded handles, and all pieces have raised floral decoration over their entire bodies except around the necks and feet. Three pieces have finials that are rather plain. There are no monograms, and the items are marked "S. Kirk and Son Sterling."

What is it?

Kirk "Repousse" tea sets have been made in an amazing variety of shapes and styles. Some were made in coin silver and some in sterling silver, some came with a vermeil or gold-plated finish, some have round handles, some have rectangular handles, some have rams'-head masks on the handles, and some have more repoussé work on them than others.

Some of the most desired of the "Repousse" tea sets incorporate elaborate landscapes into their decoration. These often feature buildings and trees, and sometimes even a fisherman sitting on the bank of a stream holding a fishing rod. These are very attractive, but they are hard to find and command a premium price in the current marketplace.

Not all pieces of Kirk "Repousse" are decorated in the same manner, and the surfaces on some examples are more fully covered with decoration than the surfaces on other examples. Early on, the repoussé decoration tended to cover the metal surface fully and there was a profusion of flowers everywhere the eye looked, but as time went on, some hollowware pieces were only three-quarters covered, others about half, and some had a partial covering that generally consisted of relatively narrow bands of repoussé flowers around rims and perhaps around the center of the body of pieces with globular shapes.

The examples pictured above are three-quarters covered, and such areas as the ends of spouts, the necks, and bases have only vestigial decoration that is nonfloral. This particular set was made during the second quarter of the 20th century.

What is it worth?

This five-piece set with three-quarter repoussé decoration should be valued for insurance purposes at $5,750. Earlier examples with bodies fully covered with repoussé can command prices that are double this figure or more if they also have landscapes.

Item 49
Reed and Barton Fish Slice, "Trajan"

Valued at $800

Knife-shaped serving piece with a wide blade that has a pierced decoration in the form of a stylized dolphin. The piece is 11 3/4 inches long and marked with the images of an eagle with its wings partially spread, the letter "R" in a shield, a lion standing on its back paws with its tail over its back, and the word "Sterling."

What is it? The marks on this piece indicate that it was manufactured by the Reed & Barton Company of Taunton, Massachusetts. This firm traces its origins to Isaac Babbitt and William W. Crossman, who established a partnership to make items from Britannia metal in 1824.

Initially, the company was very successful. By 1826, they were able to build a new facility and add steam power to run the new machinery. The company then went through several partnership changes, and in 1830, it became a joint-stock company called the Taunton Britannia Manufacturing Company.

This company failed in 1843, but three of its former employees continued the business. They were Benjamin Pratt, Henry Reed, a spinner of Britannia and pewter vessels, and Charles F. Barton, a solderer. Reed and Barton knew the manufacturing part of the business and Pratt was the salesman, and together they got the Taunton Britannia Manufacturing Company back on its feet.

After some other partnership changes, the firm became Reed and Barton around 1840. From the late 1840s to the late 1880s, Reed and Barton specialized in making silver plated flatware, but in

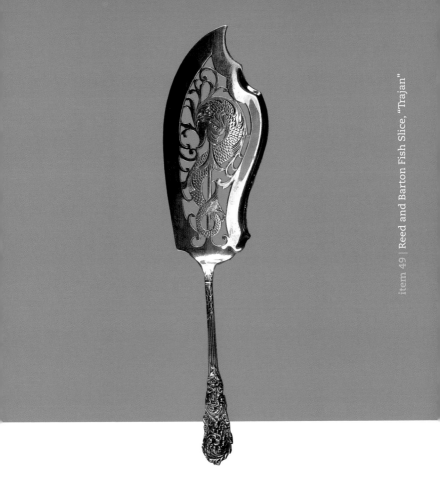

1889 they began the production of sterling silver flatware. By 1904, the manufacture of sterling silver was the biggest part of Reed and Barton's business.

The piece pictured here is a fish slice or knife used for serving fish. It is in Reed and Barton's "Trajan" pattern, which was introduced in 1892. This is a heavy, intricate pattern that is no longer made. As a general rule, it is not greatly in demand. However, a fish slice is a very uncommon part of a flatware service, and one this attractive with the intricate cutout work is highly desirable.

What is it worth?
For insurance replacement purposes, this fish slice is worth $800. A ladle in this same pattern is worth $350; a salad set, $400; and a cold-meat fork, $150. A dinner fork should be valued at $75 and a teaspoon at $40. These prices are for pieces with no monograms. Monogrammed items are somewhat lower in value.

Mark used by Reed and Barton

American Metalware   141

Item 50
Reed and Barton Flatware, "Francis I"

Valued at $6,394; $13,570

Sterling silver flatware service for twelve, consisting of twelve each of 7 3/4-inch forks, 6 1/8-inch salad forks, 9 5/8-inch knives, 4 1/4-inch demitasse spoons, 6-inch round-bowl cream soup spoons, 6 5/8-inch oval-bowl soup spoons, 5 7/8-inch individual butter spreaders, 7 3/4-inch ice-tea spoons, and 5 5/8-inch oyster forks; twenty-four 5 7/8-inch teaspoons; and an assortment of serving pieces: three 8 3/8-inch table/serving spoons; one 6 1/8-inch sugar shell, one 8 1/4-inch tomato server, one 9 1/4-inch cold-meat fork (pictured), one 7-inch master butter knife, one 6 7/8-inch gravy ladle, one 16-inch punch ladle with a silver bowl, and one 10 1/8-inch pie and cake server with a stainless steel blade. This is a total of 141 pieces, and there are no monograms. The pieces are marked with an "R" flanked by a lion and an eagle.

What is it?

As was mentioned in the discussion about the fish slice, the marks indicate that this set of sterling silver flatware was made by the Reed and Barton Company of Taunton, Massachusetts. The elaborate pattern is called "Francis I," and it is one of the most popular silver flatware patterns of all time.

Introduced in 1907, "Francis I" is considered a premium pattern and is highly sought, not so much by collectors but by those who want to use it to set an elegant table. Many upscale brides chose "Francis I" to be their wedding silver, and as a result, it has taken on heirloom status.

An incredibly wide range of pieces are available in this pattern. Those who feel the need may add such items as strawberry forks, butter picks, sherbet spoons, pasta servers, waffle servers, petit-four servers, cheese scoops, fish slices, and a myriad of other serving pieces.

What is it worth?

Replacements.com:

a.	Twelve 7 3/4-inch dinner forks @ $66 each	$ 792
b.	Twelve 6 1/8-inch salad forks @ $42 each	$ 504
c.	Twenty-four 5 7/8-inch teaspoons @ $24 each	$ 576
d.	Twelve 9 5/8-inch dinner knives @ $48 each	$ 576
e.	Twelve 4 1/4-inch demitasse spoons (coffee spoons) @ $30 each	$ 360
f.	Twelve 6-inch round-bowl cream soup spoon @ $36 each	$ 432
g.	Twelve 5 5/8-inch oval-bowl soup spoons @ $46 each	$ 552
h.	Twelve 5 7/8-inch individual butter spreaders @ $34 each	$ 408
i.	Twelve 7 3/4-inch ice-tea spoons @ $45 each	$ 540
j.	Twelve 5 5/8-inch oyster forks @ $40 each	$ 480
k.	Three 8 3/8-inch table/serving spoons @ $100 each	$ 300
l.	One 6 1/8-inch sugar shell @ $40 each	$ 40
m.	One tomato server @ $110 each	$ 110
n.	One 9 1/4-inch cold-meat fork @ $120 each	$ 120
o.	One 7-inch master butter knife @ $34 each	$ 34
p.	One 6 7/8-inch gravy ladle @ $100 each	$ 100
q.	One 16-inch punch ladle @ $400 each	$ 400
r.	One 10 1/8-inch pie and cake server @ $70 each	$ 70

TOTAL SET $ 6,394

If you should be lucky enough to have hollowware items in the "Francis I" pattern, Replacements, Ltd. lists such items as the tilt cradle kettle with stand and burner (40 troy ounces) at $25,000, a teapot (32 ounces) at $4,900, and a five-piece tea set with coffeepot, teapot, cream pitcher, sugar bowl, and waste bowl at $14,800.

Reed and Barton suggested retail prices:

a.	Twelve large dinner forks @ $120 each	$ 1,440
b.	Twelve salad forks @ $85 each	$ 1,020
c.	Twenty-four teaspoons @ $90 each	$ 2,160
d.	Twelve dinner knives @ $90 each	$ 1,080
e.	Twelve demitasse spoons (coffee spoon) @ $60 each	$ 720
f.	Twelve round-bowl cream soup spoons @ $90 each	$ 1,080
g.	Twelve oval-bowl soup spoons @ $120 each	$ 1,440
h.	Twelve long individual butter spreaders @ $70 each	$ 840
i.	Twelve ice-tea spoons @ $90 each	$ 1,080
j.	Twelve oyster forks @ $70 each	$ 840
k.	Three table/serving spoons @ $190 each	$ 570
l.	One long sugar shell @ $85	$ 85
m.	One tomato server @ $175	$ 175
n.	One cold-meat fork @ $190	$ 190
o.	One master butter knife @ $95	$ 95
p.	One gravy ladle @ $190	$ 190
q.	One punch ladle @ $480	$ 480
r.	One pie and cake server @ $85	$ 85

TOTAL SET $13,570

Item 51

Dominick and Haff Flatware, "Labors of Cupid"

Valued at $9,538

One fork from a set of flatware consisting of twelve each of 7-inch place forks, 6 1/8-inch salad forks, 9 5/8-inch dinner knives, 8 3/4-inch luncheon knives, and 5 1/2-inch seafood forks; eighteen 6 1/8-inch teaspoons; three 8 5/8-inch serving spoons; two 8 5/8-inch pierced serving spoons; one 6 1/8-inch gravy ladle; and one 9 3/8-inch pie server. The pattern is unusual, with a pierced handle decorated with a putto (plural "putti"—sometimes called a "Cupid") in the French Rococo manner. This is an assembled set, meaning that the pieces were gathered over a number of years, and some are quite old, whereas others are newer. Some of the pieces are signed "Sterling" with the initials "D. & H.," and others have three conjoined geometric figures—a rectangle with "925" in it next to a circle, which in turn is next to a diamond with a date inside. The pieces are not monogrammed.

What is it? This unusual pattern is called "Labors of Cupid," and it was first produced by the New York City firm of Dominick and Haff in 1900. Not all the designs found on the handles are alike, and the figure of the Cupids or "putti" can be found in a number of different positions engaged in various kinds of labor.

Note that the Cupid on the salad fork is shown picking flowers and putting them into a basket, whereas the Cupid on the dinner fork is shown climbing a ladder to pick fruit. The stem of each of these two forks is different as well, with the one on the flower-picking example having "C" scrolls and leaves while the stem on the fruit-picking example has a cornucopia spilling out fruit just above the tines.

It should be understood that the flower-picking example is older than the fruit-picking piece, and is a bit heavier and more detailed. This is an important point because many times there are significant differences in both weight and design between newer and older pieces of flatware in patterns that have been made over a long period of time. It is not unusual for the older items to be heavier and more detailed, whereas the newer versions may look similar but are lighter and less well made.

Dominick and Haff was established in 1872 by H. Blanchard Dominick, the descendant of a French Huguenot who had immigrated to this country in 1740, and Leroy B. Haff, who began his career in the silversmith trade by working with William Gale in the firm of Gale and North.

This firm became Gale, North and Dominick in 1868, and then Gale, Dominick and Haff in 1870. Two years later, Gale was no longer part of the partnership, and Dominick and Haff were specializing in making small pieces of silver including vinaigrettes (small decorative bottles with perforated tops used to hold aromatic substances such as smelling salts) and chatelaines (clasps or chains worn at the waist for holding keys, a watch, a purse, or in some cases, small sewing accessories such as scissors).

After a fire in 1877, the firm moved to a larger facility and expanded the number and types of silver articles they made. In 1879, Dominick and Haff bought out Adams and Shaw, another New York silver-making firm, and they were acquired by Reed and Barton in 1928.

"Labors of Cupid" is a charming pattern, but it is considered to be obsolete and the sort of thing that is associated with the dining tables of great-grandparents. Still, these pieces do command a respectable price when they can be found for sale because many people like the Cupid motifs.

What is it worth? These prices are from Replacements.com, which sells both new and old examples of this pattern.

a.	Twelve 7-inch place forks @ $119 each	$ 1,428
b.	Twelve 6 1/8-inch salad forks @ $95 each	$ 1,140
c.	Eighteen 6 1/8-inch teaspoons @ $70	$ 1,260
d.	Twelve 9 5/8-inch dinner knives @ $90 each (New)	$ 1,080
e.	Twelve 8 3/4-inch luncheon knives @ $70 each (New)	$ 840
f.	Twelve 5 1/2-inch oyster forks @ $230 each (Old)	$ 2,760
g.	Three 8 5/8-inch serving spoons @ $170 each	$ 510
h.	Two 8 5/8-inch pierced serving spoons @ $160 each	$ 320
i.	One 6 1/8-inch gravy ladle @ $120	$ 120
j.	One 9 3/8-inch pie server @ $80	$ 80

TOTAL SET $ 9,538

Item 52

Tiffany Pitcher "Wave Edge"

Valued at $5,000; $3,500

Sterling silver water pitcher, 6 7/8 inches tall. It has a globular body with a raised collar neck and a handle with gadrooning where it meets the body and the neck. A simple band of decoration around the center of the body consists of undulating lines stacked on top of one another. This motif is repeated around the neck, but is less wide. The piece is marked on the base "Tiffany & Co., Makers, Sterling Silver, 925–1000," and has a capital "M" below.

What is it?

Tiffany and Company was founded in 1837 as Tiffany and Young by Charles Lewis Tiffany and John B. Young. They were basically a stationery, fancy goods, and bric-a-brac store carrying items such as fans, Chinese accessories, umbrellas, and desks. They were initially at 259 West Broadway in New York City, and at this time they did not make silver objects themselves, but purchased their stock from John Chandler Moore, who had been a silversmith in New York City since 1827.

In 1841, the firm became Tiffany, Young & Ellis. In 1853, Charles Tiffany took over and the business became Tiffany and Company. Two years earlier, in 1851, John C. Moore retired and his son Edward C. Moore took over and entered into an arrangement with Tiffany to make silverware exclusively for Tiffany. That same year (1851), Tiffany introduced the English sterling standard (925 parts of silver to every 1,000 parts of metal) to America, which eventually became the accepted standard for solid silver made in the United States.

In 1868, Tiffany and Company was incorporated and purchased the Moore silverware factory. Edward C. Moore became a member of the Tiffany board, and until his death in 1891, a capital "M" was used as part of the Tiffany mark. After that the initial of the company's president was stamped under the mark, with "C's," "T's," and "M's" most commonly found. The pattern on this pitcher is called "Wave Edge." It was first made in 1884 and is currently still in production.

What is it worth?

According to Replacements Ltd., this mid-20th-century "Wave Edge" pattern pitcher should be valued at $5,000. Tiffany and Company reports that the suggested retail price for a new "Wave Edge" pitcher is $3,500.

Set of sterling silver flatware
consisting of twelve each of 8-inch
dinner forks, 6 7/8-inch salad forks,
7 1/8-inch soup spoons, 9 3/8-inch dinner knives, and oyster forks;
eighteen 6 1/8-inch teaspoons; three 8 5/8-inch serving spoons; a two-
piece salad serving set, and an oyster server (pictured). The pattern has
a ruffled shell-shaped device at the terminal of each handle, with ripples
and wavelike forms running down the edge (these wavelike forms could
also be interpreted as leaves). There are no monograms on these pieces,
and each item is marked "Tiffany and Company."

What is it?
Although the pattern does not much resemble the design of the pitcher
pictured just before this, both are in fact Tiffany's "Wave Edge." This
pattern has been in production since 1884. These flatware pieces are
still available from Tiffany, but many heirloom sets are also available.

What is it worth?
Once again, because this pattern is currently available from the
manufacturer and from secondary market suppliers, we quote both the
retail prices from the secondary market (Replacements, Ltd.), and the
manufacturer's suggested retail value. It should be noted that the
examples under discussion are not monogrammed. Monogrammed
flatware often brings far less on the secondary market than those
without monograms, but the demand for Tiffany's "Wave Edge" is so
high that the deduction for monograms is very small if there is any at all.

Replacements.com:

a.	Twelve 8-inch dinner forks @ $150 each	$ 1,800
b.	Twelve 6 7/8-inch salad forks @ $180 each	$ 2,160
c.	Eighteen 6 1/8-inch teaspoons @ $75 each	$ 1,350
d.	Twelve 7 1/8-inch soup spoons @ $110 each	$ 1,320
e.	Twelve 9 3/8-inch dinner knives @ $150 each	$ 1,800
f.	Twelve oyster forks @ $150 each	$ 1,800
g.	Three 8 5/8-inch serving spoons @ $140 each	$ 420
h.	One two-piece salad set (large fork and spoon) @ $1,460	$ 1,460
i.	One oyster ladle @ $640	$ 640
		TOTAL SET $12,950

Tiffany and Company's suggested retail:

a.	Twelve dinner forks @ $150 each	$ 1,800
b.	Twelve salad forks @ $115 each	$ 1,380
c.	Twelve dinner knives @ $135 each	$ 1,620
d.	Two serving spoons @ $200 each	$ 400

Other prices for new production "Wave Edge" flatware were not available
from the manufacturer.

item 52 | Tiffany Pitcher "Wave Edge"

Item 53
Tiffany Tilt Cradle Hot-Water Kettle,
"Chrysanthemum"

Valued at $20,000

Tilt cradle hot-water kettle with burner. The kettle has a handle with art nouveau–style curves. The lid has a finial in the form of a chrysanthemum bud, and the spout is surrounded with flower buds and leaves. The kettle itself has a lobed body and rests in a cradle that allows it to tilt safely and dispense hot water. The sides of the cradle that hold the pot are decorated with raised flowers and leaves, and the feet on the base are decorated with leaves and flower buds as well. The piece is marked "Tiffany & Co. Makers Sterling Silver 925–1000" and a cursive "M." In addition, the kettle is monogrammed.

What is it? Tea sets were—and are—often made with a number of different pieces. There is usually a teapot and a coffeepot plus a cream pitcher, a sugar bowl, and perhaps a waste bowl. Solid sterling trays that match the set are very unusual (unless the set is Mexican) as are elaborate hot-water kettles held in tilt cradle frames.

These devices are the height of elegance, and they were generally made for sets that were used on a regular basis rather than for sets that led a more ornamental life. The hot-water kettle was used to hold a reservoir of hot water that was kept warm with the burner underneath and then poured into the teapot when tea was to be brewed. Sets with hot-water kettles often had waste bowls as well. These were meant to receive the used, wet leaves from the tea-making process after the beverage was brewed.

This particular hot-water kettle is in Tiffany's "Chrysanthemum" pattern, which was introduced in 1880 and is still in production. This is a particularly beautiful example of a tilt cradle hot-water kettle, but the monogram on its surface hurts the value just a bit.

What is it worth?

This vintage kettle is valued at $20,000, and other pieces of Tiffany "Chrysanthemum" pattern sterling silver are also quite valuable. A simple creamer, for example, is priced at $1,880 on Replacements.com, a small teapot is $8,000, and an asparagus dish is $4,000. Tiffany and Company reports that the suggested retail price of a new "Chrysanthemum" hot-water kettle is $11,000.

Related item

Fork from a set of flatware consisting of twelve each of 7 1/2-inch dinner forks, 9 3/4-inch dinner knives, 4-inch demitasse spoons, 6 7/8-inch oval soup spoons, 6-inch oyster forks; eighteen 5-inch teaspoons; two 8 1/2-inch pierced serving spoons; and one pair of sugar tongs. The pieces are marked "Tiffany & Co. Makers" and "Sterling." The pattern itself is characterized by a three-dimensional chrysanthemum blossom at the terminal of each handle with an oval cartouche below framed by leaves and flower buds. The pieces are not monogrammed.

What is it?

Tiffany's "Chrysanthemum" pattern flatware has been made since 1880. The pieces in this service are not monogrammed, but those that do bear their original owners' initials are 10 to 15 percent less valuable than the prices quoted here.

What is it worth?

Since "Chrysanthemum" is still being made, we quote retail prices found on the secondary market at Replacements.com and the suggested retail value from Tiffany and Company.

Replacements.com:

a.	Twelve 7 1/2-inch dinner forks @ $240 each	$ 2,880
b.	Twelve 9 3/4-inch dinner knives @ $260 each	$ 3,120
c.	Eighteen 5 3/4-inch teaspoons @ $120 each	$ 2,160
d.	Twelve 4-inch demitasse spoons @ $90 each	$ 1,080
e.	Twelve 6 7/8-inch oval soup spoons @ $220 each	$ 2,640
f.	Twelve 6-inch oyster forks @ $130 each	$ 1,560
g.	Two 8 1/2-inch pierced serving spoons @ $300 each	$ 600
h.	One pair of sugar tongs @ $300	$ 300
		TOTAL SET $14,340

Tiffany and Company suggested retail:

a.	Twelve dinner forks @ $155 each	$ 1,860
b.	Twelve dinner knives @ $135 each	$ 1,620
c.	Eighteen teaspoons @ $125 each	$ 2,250
d.	Two pierced serving spoons @ $210 each	$ 420

Other prices on new production "Chrysanthemum" pattern flatware were not available from the manufacturer.

Item 54

Tiffany Demitasse Coffee Set,
"English King"

Valued at $6,000

Demitasse coffee set consisting of a
circular tray, a coffeepot, a cream pitcher,
and a covered sugar bowl. The pieces are
primarily decorated with raised shell-
like devices, and there is a monogram.
Each piece is footed and marked "Tiffany
and Co. Makers Sterling Silver."

What is it? The pattern of this set is called "English King."
Although the flatware in this pattern was first produced in 1885 the
hollowware may have been available as early as 1870. This classic
pattern is still in production today.

It is unusual to find a matching sterling silver tray with regular-size
tea sets, but for small demitasse sets such as this one, the tray is
standard.

What is it worth? The insurance replacement value
on this set is $6,000.

Item 55
Gebelein Flatware

What is it? At first glance, these pieces look like they could be earlier than they really are. The design of these pieces and the way they are signed (apart from the word "sterling") make them appear to be early 19th century, but they are early 20th century.

George Christian Gebelein was born in Bavaria in 1878 and came to the United States when he was just a year old. At the age of fourteen, in 1892, he was apprenticed to the firm of Goodnow and Jenks, a Boston firm that was the successor to Kennard and Jenks, which was bought by Gorham in 1880. In late 1897, Gebelein went to work for Tiffany and Company at their new factory in Forest Hills, New Jersey. He left Tiffany and New Jersey to move to Concord, New Hampshire, where he was employed by the William B. Durgin Company, which had been making silver since 1853. Durgin had built his business by making a quantity of spoons, packing them in a satchel or small trunk and selling them from a wagon as he traveled the countryside.

Valued at $10,575

One hundred thirty-two flatware pieces marked with an incised "Gebelein," "Sterling," and "Boston." Set consists of twelve each: teaspoons, knives with stainless-steel handles, soup spoons, demitasse spoons, dessert forks, and ice-tea spoons plus twenty-four forks, thirteen butter spreaders, eleven oyster forks, a large fork and spoon salad set, two sauce ladles, a cold-meat fork, three serving spoons, two sugar shells, a cake server, and an ice-cream server. About 164 troy ounces. The pattern features an embossed basket of fruit and shell design.

Around 1903, Gebelein became a member of the Handicraft Shop of Boston, which is associated with the Boston Society of Arts and Crafts, the oldest nonprofit crafts organization in the United States still in existence. In 1909, he opened up his own shop at 79 Chestnut Street in Boston's Beacon Hill section. There he became known for fine handmade reproductions of early silver and for adaptations of earlier patterns.

Gebelein also made hand-hammered copper bowls lined with silver as well as some silver plated and pewter items. He died in 1945, but his tradition of excellence was continued by his son J. Herbert Gebelein, who was also known for the quality of his work. This particular flatware service is early 20th century.

What is it worth? This set sold at auction in February 2005 for $10,575.

Item 56

Gorham Candelabra, "Buttercup"

Valued at $380

Three-cup candelabra with a base that is marked with an anchor flanked by a lion and a Gothic capital letter "G," the word "Sterling," and a small hexagon with the number "2" inside. The candelabra is 8 1/2 inches tall and has a weighted base. The base is decorated with raised flowers and leaves, and the rest is undecorated. It is not monogrammed.

What is it? The Gorham Corporation of Providence, Rhode
Island, traces its beginnings to Jabez Gorham, who was born in
Providence in 1792. He was apprenticed at age fourteen to Ne-
hemiah Dodge, who worked from approximately 1790 to 1824.
After finishing his seven-year apprenticeship, Gorham went into
partnership with several other young silversmiths and opened a
manufacturing facility for making small items of silver including
what came to be known as "Gorham chain," which is said to have
been the best being made at the time.

In the 1830s, Gorham joined Henry L. Webster to establish Gorham
and Webster (1831–37), where he (Gorham) was particularly known
for making spoons. After another name change, Gorham's son John
joined the company, and from 1841 to 1850 it was known as Jabez
Gorham and Son.

John Gorham's great contribution to the company was his
recognition of the importance of machinery and mechaniza-
tion to the future of the silver-making industry. The idea at the
time was to augment the hand craftsmanship with the assistance of machines; and when he could not find a machine to
do what he needed, he designed one to accomplish the purpose he had in mind.

Jabez Gorham retired in 1847, and John Gorham took a man named
Thurber as his partner from 1850 to 1852. The firm became Gorham
and Company in 1852. In 1863, Rhode Island granted a charter to
the company as the Gorham Manufacturing Company, a name it
retained until 1961, when it became the Gorham Corporation.

Gorham eventually became one of the giants in the manufacturing of American silver. Over the years, it gobbled up many of its
competitors including the Alvin Silver Company, the William B.
Durgin Company, Woods and Hughes, and the Whiting Manufacturing Company.

Gorham Manufacturing began a huge number of patterns, and one
of its late-19th-century patterns, "Buttercup," is still popular
today. This floral design, which was first made in 1899, features
three raised blossoms at the terminal of the flatware pieces. The
sides are festooned with more blossoms and "C" scrolls that come
together to make another grouping of three blossoms. These blossoms are said to resemble buttercups, but that is really a matter of
some interpretation.

The candelabra pictured here is classically simple with a garland
of buttercups arranged around the stem. The base is weighted

with cement to give the candelabra stability and to keep it from tipping over when tall candles are burning in the cups. In addition, the cement reduced the amount of silver that had to be used, thereby keeping the consumer's cost down.

As noted in the description, this candelabra has the standard Gorham marks on it, but it also has a hexagon with a "2" inside. This is a date letter and indicates that this piece was manufactured in 1962. Gorham started a dating system on its hollowware in 1868, when it marked pieces with an "A" to indicate the year of production. The company ran the alphabet to "Q" in 1884, and then began using symbols such as a boar's head for 1885, a bell for 1900, a pipe for 1911, an acorn for 1924, and an airplane for 1927.

This system was discontinued in 1933 and not resumed until 1941, when the numeral "1" appeared inside a cube to indicate 1941. A "2" inside a cube indicates 1942 and so on. In the 1950s the system was continued, except the cube for the forties became a pentagon. No number inside the pentagon indicated that the piece was made in 1950, and numerals through 9 indicated the specific year within the decade.

In the sixties, the shape was a hexagon, and therefore, the "2" in the hexagon on this "Buttercup" candelabra tells us the piece was made in 1962. In the seventies, the shape became a heptagon, and the system continued.

What is it worth?

When it comes to candlesticks and candelabra, most collectors prefer pairs to single pieces. This single candelabra is valued at $380 by Replacements, Ltd., but if there had been a pair, the price would have more than doubled to $850 for the two. Other hollowware pieces in this pattern include a four-piece tea set (teapot, coffeepot, cream pitcher, sugar bowl) for $3,000, and a five-piece set (a four-piece set plus a waste bowl) is $3,600. A large, 12-inch, five-cup candelabra is $950, and a salt and pepper shaker set is $160.

NOTE: "Buttercup" hollowware was made in silver plate as well as sterling silver. Silver plated examples should have the letters "E P" as part of the mark along with an anchor and either the name "Gorham" or the initials "G M Co." In silver plate, a five-piece tea set with a tray is $1,400, and a 22-inch tray is $750. There is no indication that the company is currently making the sterling candelabra shown here.

Related item

Fork from an extensive set of flatware, marked "Gorham" with three punches, featuring a lion, an anchor, and a Gothic letter "G" plus the word "Sterling." The pattern itself is composed of three blossoms at the terminal of each handle, with flowers and "C" scrolls cascading down the sides to a tight grouping of three blossoms and leaves. The set consists of twelve each of 7 1/2-inch place forks, 6 3/8-inch salad forks, 9 1/8-inch place knives, 4 1/2-inch demitasse spoons, 6 3/4-inch oval-bowl soup spoons, 7 1/2-inch iced-tea spoons, and 5 1/2-inch seafood forks; eighteen 5-inch teaspoons; four 8 3/8-inch serving spoons; one 6-inch sugar spoon; one 6 1/8-inch gravy ladle; one pickle/olive fork; one 6 1/2-inch cheese cleaver; one 6 3/4-inch master butter knife, one 10 5/8-inch pie and cake server with stainless steel blade; and one large roast carving set with a sharpening steel. There are no monograms.

What is it?

As noted earlier, the Gorham "Buttercup" pattern has been in production since 1899, and many brides have chosen it as their wedding silver. It is important to understand that at one time, Gorham made its flatware in as many as five different weights. There is the "Trade weight," which was marked with a "T"; Medium weight, marked with an "M"; Heavy weight, marked with an "H"; and Extra Heavy weight, marked with an "EH."

There was also a standard weight, which had no mark indicating the weight. When the heavier pieces can be found, collectors prefer them to the lighter. When assembling a set, caution should be exercised to buy pieces all of the same weight. The pieces detailed above are all standard weight.

What is it worth?

"Buttercup" is currently in production, so once again we list prices available on the secondary market and the suggested retail prices from Gorham.

Replacements.com:

a.	Twelve 7 1/2-inch place forks @ $40 each	$ 480
b.	Twelve 6 3/8-inch salad forks @ $43 each	$ 516
c.	Eighteen 5 3/4-inch teaspoons @ $24 each	$ 432
d.	Twelve 9 1/8-inch place knives @ $30 each	$ 360
e.	Twelve 4 1/2-inch demitasse spoons @ $32	$ 384
f.	Twelve 6 3/4-inch oval-bowl soup spoons @ $44 each	$ 528
g.	Twelve 7 1/2-inch iced-tea spoons @ $40 each	$ 480
h.	Twelve 5 1/2-inch seafood forks @ $30 each	$ 360
i.	Four 8 3/8-inch serving spoons @ $70 each	$ 280

j.	One 6-inch sugar spoon @ $44	$ 44
k.	One 6 1/8-inch gravy ladle @ $90	$ 90
l.	One pickle/olive fork @ $40	$ 40
m.	One 6 1/2-inch cheese cleaver @ $50	$ 50
n.	One 6 3/4-inch master butter knife @ $34	$ 34
o.	One 10 5/8-inch pie and cake server @ $50	$ 50
p.	One large roast carving set with sharpening steel @ $170	$ 170
	TOTAL SET	$ 4,298

Gorham suggested retail prices:

a.	Twelve place forks @ $69 each	$ 828
b.	Twelve salad forks @ $68 each	$ 816
c.	Eighteen teaspoons @ $68 each	$ 1,224
d.	Twelve place knives @ $66 each	$ 792
e.	Twelve demitasse spoons @ $66 each	$ 792
f.	Twelve oval-bowl soup spoons @ $68 each	$ 816
g.	Twelve iced-tea spoons @ $68 each	$ 816
h.	Twelve seafood forks @ $66.50 each	$ 798
i.	Four serving spoons @ $138 each	$ 552
j.	One sugar spoon @ $68	$ 68
k.	One gravy ladle @ $138	$ 138
l.	One pickle/olive fork	N/A
m.	One cheese cleaver	N/A
n.	One master butter knife @ $66	$ 66
o.	One pie and cake server @ $56	$ 56
p.	One large roast carving set with sharpening steel @ $402	$ 402
	TOTAL SET	$ 8,164

Item 57
Simon, Bro. and Company Match Safe

Valued at $125

Small box with hinged lid. The body is decorated with raised leaf tendrils and "C" scrolls with a heart-shaped center surrounded by raised rays. On the bottom is an arched series of raised ridges. Inside the top cover is the word "sterling" with an "S" inside a square device with a pointed lower end. The piece is 2 1/2 inches long by 1 1/2 inches at the widest point and is monogrammed "A. F. B." in the heart-shaped area on one side of the case.

What is it?

As anyone who has ever watched one of those shows about people trying to stay alive on a desert island or in some forsaken piece of jungle know, it is hard to light a fire if you do not have a match. For our ancestors, it was a daily struggle to keep a flame handy to light a candle or ignite fuel to make a fire.

Then in 1827, an English chemist and druggist named John Walker put together a concoction of potassium chloride, antimony sulphide, and gum and put it on a stick. When the end of the stick with the chemicals on it was rubbed against a piece of sandpaper, it would ignite, and the friction match was born.

It sounds like a simple invention to us. But this device was hailed by some as one of the greatest discoveries of the era because it made life so much easier for the average person who no longer had to worry about where his or her next spark of fire was coming from. These early matches, however, were more than a bit unstable, and care had to be taken as to where and how they were stored.

Special match holders proliferated, and wall-mounted units were found next to the stove in the kitchen and the fireplace in the parlor in all but the most impoverished homes. Even though the "safety" match was invented in 1855, it was still thought unsafe to carry unprotected matches on one's person because the phrase "liar, liar pants on fire" could take on a real and disastrous meaning.

Metal match safes solved this problem. They were made in a wide range of styles from a wide variety of metals. Some were very simple with company advertisements on them while others were figural and came in the shape of anything from a boot to the profile of a Japanese geisha. There were also match safes with cupids or putti on them, and match safes with raised hunting or fishing scenes were popular.

In addition, match safes sometimes incorporated cigar cutters and hidden compartments. The presence of these details usually raises the value of a match safe a bit. Examples can be found in brass, tin, silver plate, brass plated with nickel, and sterling silver. As the marks on the piece pictured here suggest, this particular match safe was made in sterling silver by Simon, Bro. and Company of Philadelphia.

This company was established in 1840 by George W. Simon, who later took his brother Peter B. Simon, and his sons John, Frederick, and Edwin into the firm. George Simon was born in 1819 and entered the silver-making trade specializing in crafting thimbles and pencils. Later in the 19th century, the company widened its product line and began making cane tops and umbrella heads plus comb tops and other accessory items, tea sets, and flatware.

The Alvin Manufacturing Company of Providence, Rhode Island, bought them out in 1908.

What is it worth? The nonfigural and nonpictorial nature of this match safe keeps the monetary value down, but there are collectors who are interested in antique items that incorporate heart themes. The fact that this piece is sterling silver helps the monetary worth, and the insurance replacement value of this piece is $125.

SILVER
PLATE

Item 58

Pairpoint Basket

Valued at $400

Basket, silvered metal, marked "Pairpoint Mfg. Company" over a diamond-shaped device with a "P" inside. Under this is "Quadruple Plate" and "81247." The piece is 12 1/2 inches long by 10 inches tall at the swing handle. The body and the handle are pierced with a floral decoration, and the piece is monogrammed with a "B."

What is it? The Pairpoint Corporation was organized in 1880 by internationally famous silver designer Thomas J. Pairpoint, who had served his apprenticeship in Paris and had worked for the prestigious firm of Lambert and Rawlings in London. Upon returning to the United States, Pairpoint became chief designer for the Gorham Manufacturing Company of Providence, Rhode Island.

Pairpoint was one of the first craftsmen in this country to think of silver as an art medium. He had a reputation for work in the Victorian Renaissance Revival substyle, which, as the name suggests, was based on neoclassical designs derived from the Italian Re-

naissance. Later, however, much of the production at Pairpoint's factory was based on Eastlake and Art Nouveau designs.

In 1877, Pairpoint left Gorham and joined the Meriden Britannia Company, in Meriden, Connecticut, as a designer and modeler. Just two years later, in 1879, Pairpoint left Meriden to form his own company in the seaport town of New Bedford, Massachusetts. The facility was located next door to the Mt. Washington Glass Company, which made some of the best American colored art glass of the time.

Inexplicably, Pairpoint left his company on April 1, 1885. He said at the time that he was going to start another manufacturing facility but never did, and he died seventeen years later, in 1902.

Typical mark
used by the
Pairpoint
Manufacturing
Company

Initially, the Pairpoint Manufacturing Company specialized in making coffin fittings and other types of metalware. Silver plated objects were widely made but some sterling silver was produced as well—mainly as mountings for high-quality pieces of glass.

In 1894, the Pairpoint Manufacturing Company bought its neighbor, the Mt. Washington Glass Company, and the combined concerns began producing such things as silver plated hollowware, lamps, stemware, and even finely painted china, using "blanks" (i.e., undecorated pieces of white china) from makers in Limoges, France.

In the 20th century Pairpoint struggled. The name was changed to the Pairpoint Corporation in 1900, and the company closed for a time during the Great Depression. Revival occurred—mainly in the glass-making portion of the business—and today, Pairpoint can be found making glass in Sandwich, Massachusetts, which is located at the base of Cape Cod.

The silver plated basket pictured here is very much in the Art Nouveau style and can be dated to the last decade of the 19th century, circa 1895. The floral pierced work is very attractive to collectors. and these are sometimes referred to as cake baskets. This is something of a misnomer because their most common use was to hold either fruit or bread.

The term "quadruple plate" found on the bottom refers to the amount of silver that was used in the silver plating process. Collectors sometimes find pieces marked "A1," "Double Plate," "Triple Plate," or "Quadruple Plate." "A1" refers to standard silver plate and means that to plate 144 teaspoons, 2 troy ounces of pure silver were used; for "Double Plate," 4 troy ounces of silver were used; and for "Triple Plate," 6 troy ounces were required.

"Quadruple Plate" used 8 troy ounces of silver to plate those 144 teaspoons, and is the thickest, best-quality silver plate commonly found by collectors. It should be understood, however, that this coating is still relatively thin and wears off rather easily with decades of zealous polishing. Silver plate that has had all its precious metal polished off can be very unattractive, and prices for these pieces can be significantly depressed.

This Pairpoint basket has been resilvered, a process that does not harm the value of an antique piece of silver plate unless it is poorly done. On occasion, owners will send out a cherished family heirloom to be resilvered and it will come back looking like a thin film of silvery foil has been adhered to the surface.

This is an eyesore and not the way a piece of resilvered silver plate should look. Those who are contemplating having some resilvering done should make sure that the firm doing the job will supply an old looking patina, is reputable, and stands behind its work.

What is it worth? The resilvering on this basket looks a little thick and some of the details have been blurred a bit, but this does not detract greatly from the value. The insurance replacement value is $400.

Item 59
Barbour Vase

Valued at $250

Eighteen-inch-tall vase decorated with flowers in a basket and floral sprays. It has a squared form and is 18 inches tall. There are some dents, and the piece is inscribed "Little" and dated 1928. It is signed on the bottom "Barbour S. P. Co." in a half circle mark and "International Silver Company" and "3347."

What is it? The Barbour Silver Company was founded in 1892 by Samuel L. Barbour, Isaac Steane, and J. L. Daigleish. The company, which was in Hartford, Connecticut, primarily made silver plated wares. At the time, competition in this type of manufacturing was very tough, and the Barbour Silver Company soon joined with many other small, New England–based metal-fabricating firms to form the giant International Silver Company.

Mark found on this Barbour Silver Company vase

The Meriden Britannia Company is said to have been the driving force behind the creation of International Silver, which came into being in November 1898. The list of formerly independent companies that joined this amalgamation was quite lengthy, and the Barbour Silver Company became "Factory A" of this new enterprise.

In addition to Barbour, the new company included a number of facilities started by the famous Rogers Brothers, plus Holmes and Edwards, the Middletown Plate Company, the Meriden Silver Plate Company, and others.

Over the years, International Silver used more than fifty trade names and made a wide variety of both silver plated and sterling silver wares. In 1984, the company was sold to Katy Industries, Inc., which already owned Wallace Silversmiths, and the name of the company was changed to Wallace International Silversmiths. As part of International Silver, the Barbour Silver Company's Hartford, Connecticut, facility was closed and the company was moved to Meriden, Connecticut, where it reopened in the buildings formerly used by the Meriden Silver Plate Company.

The marks on the vase pictured here tell its story. These back stamps tell us that this piece was made by the Barbour Silver Company after it became part of the International Silver Company. A little further research reveals that Barbour did not use its frequently encountered half circle trademark until around 1921, and the 1928 date seen on this piece is probably close to its date of manufacture.

Unfortunately, this piece is monogrammed, but the word "Little" is very small and is easily overlooked. Still, this monogram reduces the value of the vase by as much as 25 percent.

What is it worth? The insurance replacement value is $250.

Item 60
Middletown Plate Company Jam Jar

Valued at $85

Covered cuplike vessel with a floral knob on the lid. The round cylindrical body is engraved with floral motifs and embossed scrolls around the rim and base. There is a rope twist handle, and the base has a round hole in the bottom. It is 3 5/8 inches tall and has a 3 1/4-inch diameter. The piece is marked "Middletown Plate" with the representations of scales and "Quadruple Plate."

What is it?

Why would anyone put a large hole in the bottom of a perfectly good container so that it could hold neither a liquid such as mustard nor a solid such as sugar? This looks like a perfectly good condiment jar that has been ruined, but in actuality, it is the way it is supposed to be, and the large, gaping hole has an easily explained purpose.

Mark found on the Middletown Plate Co. jam jar

This silver plated container was made after packaged food became available to many American consumers and was designed to hide the fact that the lady of the house was serving store-bought jam instead of her own homemade confection. The idea was to take the jar of jam that had been purchased at the store and surreptitiously slip it inside this fancy container. When it was placed on the table for guests to enjoy, no unsightly jar with its paper label could be seen, and all that was visible was the fancy outer container. When the meal was finished, a finger was inserted in the convenient hole in the bottom and the commercial jam jar was pushed out to be recovered and stored. Examples that are a little taller than this one were designed to hold condensed milk cans and also disguise what they actually were.

The piece pictured here was made by the Middletown Plate Company of Middletown, Connecticut, which was founded by Edward Payne and Henry Bullard in 1864. However, they did not adopt the name Middletown Plate Company until 1866. This company continued to operate in Middletown until 1899, when like many others became part of the International Silver Company.

The company moved to Meriden, Connecticut, in June 1899, and after that, the products they made were marked with the trade name Superior Silver Company. Before the move to Meriden, this had been the designation used by Middleton on its lower-priced lines, but after joining International, the old mark with the scales and the name Middletown Plate Company was dropped.

This means that this jam jar was made pre-1899, and is probably circa 1890. It has lost almost all of its original silver plating, and only the dark gray Britannia metal base is now in evidence. Many collectors think that this is unsightly, and it will reduce the value a bit.

What is it worth?

The insurance replacement value for this jam jar is $85. Properly resilvered, that value should rise to $125.

Item 61

Derby Silver Company Creamer

Valued at $50

Small silver plated pitcher with a V-shaped handle and decorated with a band of sphinx, palm trees, and towers under the rim. On the body are representations of Japanese-style fans and foliage. The piece is 6 5/8 inches tall, and not monogrammed. The silver plate itself is in poor condition and marked with the name "Derby Silver Company" and "Quadruple Plate."

What is it? The Derby Silver Company was founded in Birmingham, Connecticut, in 1873. Initially, they specialized in flatware, but they gradually dropped this in favor of silver plated hollowware and dresser items such as brush-and-comb sets. They also made sterling silver flatware and decorative wares.

The production of sterling silver ceased around 1895, and like so many other Connecticut-based makers of silver-plated items, Derby joined the International Silver Company in 1898. The Derby Silver Company continued to operate in Derby until 1933, when it was moved to Meriden, Connecticut. Much of their later production is impressed with a half circle mark similar to the one used by the Barbour Silver Company, also part of International Silver.

The cream pitcher shown here was once part of a larger tea and coffee service, but this is the only piece from the set to have sur-

vived. This single item would be of very little interest to collectors if not for the exotic Egyptian-style decoration seen in the band around the body. The other decoration found on this creamer— particularly the fans and the foliage—are in the Victorian Eastlake style, and these motifs help date this piece to circa 1885.

This creamer is really a sad "orphan" with all of its companion pieces and original silver plating gone. Even though it is approximately 120 years old, any monetary value it has is due solely to the decoration.

What is it worth? The insurance replacement value for this cream pitcher is $50 in this condition. Professionally resilvered that value would rise to $75.

Item 62
Reed and Barton Tea Set

What is it? The history of the Reed and Barton Company of Taunton, Massachusetts, has been discussed at length in the section on sterling silver on page 141. In addition to making sterling silver, Reed and Barton also manufactured silver plate, gold electroplate, and pewter.

Between 1928 and 1957, Reed and Barton stamped a date letter or figure into all its hollowware. In 1928, the figure was an acorn. This was followed in 1929 with the representation of a torch, in 1934 with a swan, in 1937 a ship, in 1942 a "V" (for "Victory"?), in 1947 a pair of scales, in 1949 a ringed planet, in 1956 a heart, and in

Valued at $1,200

Silver plated tea service consisting of a hot-water urn, teapot, coffeepot, cream pitcher, sugar bowl, and waste bowl. The hot-water urn is 18 inches tall, the coffeepot is 11 1/2 inches tall, and the sugar bowl is 9 1/4 inches tall. The pieces are not monogrammed, and the silver plate is in excellent condition. Each piece is marked "Manufactured by Reed and Barton" accompanied by a small representation of an ax or hatchet.

1957 an arrow. In 1931, the symbol was an ax or a hatchet, which is the date symbol found on the tea set shown here.

This tea set is desirable because it is so extensive and has a hot-water urn. Collectors would prefer that it had its original matching tray, but that piece was not purchased as part of the original set or has been lost over time. The silver plating on this set is in excellent condition, and that is a big plus for both the aesthetic and the monetary value.

What is it worth? The insurance replacement value for this set is $1,200.

Glossary

ALLOY
Generally, an alloy is a metal composed of two other metals that are homogeneous, with the atoms of one replacing or occupying interstitial positions between the atoms of the other. Sterling silver, for example, is an alloy of silver and copper, with the copper added to make the silver less soft.

APPRENTICE
A person who is bound by a legal agreement or indenture to work for a craftsman or artist for a given period of time—usually seven years—in return for instruction in the craft. In many cases, the apprenticeship began at age thirteen or fourteen and the apprentice was taken in as part of the craftsman's household and given room and board while he learned all the particulars of the trade. The apprentice was basically a trainee who provided labor with little or no remuneration beyond food, shelter, and an education.

ART NOUVEAU
A decorative style that originated in France in the 1880s. It remained in fashion through the first decade of the 20th century but was out of fashion by the beginning of World War I. Art Nouveau was largely based on organic forms such as plants, animals, and the human figure. This style abhorred the straight line and widely employed the sensuous curved lines found in nature, such as the twining tendrils of vines and the curls found in a woman's hair.

ASSAY
The process of determining the purity of metals. In the case of silver and gold, it is done to determine the amount of base metal that is present. This was done in some cases by using a touchstone, which is a hard black stone such as jasper or basalt. Acid of a known type and strength was put on the stone and the stone was drawn across the metal surface in an inconspicuous spot to leave a streak. This color of the streak varied depending on the purity and content of the metal (gold, silver, platinum), and the streak on the specimen being tested was then compared to streaks on pieces of known purity, thereby determining the purity and/or composition of the test piece. Other methods, such as cupellation, were also used to assay metals.

BOBECHE
A collar of glass, ceramic, or metal with a hole in the middle that allows it to be placed around a candle to catch the wax drippings. These are also used to hold prisms.

BRASS
An alloy of copper and zinc that is typically more than 50 percent copper. White brass, however, is more than 50 percent zinc and is very brittle. Brass that is 90 percent copper and 10 percent zinc is somewhat red in color because the color of the copper predominates. Brass that is 83 percent copper and 17 percent zinc has a very golden color. Brass is harder than copper; and in ancient times, it may have been made with tin (see "Bronze"). The metal we know as brass originated around the 1500s.

BRAZIER
A maker of brass items.

BRIGHT CUT
A type of engraving that was popular in the late 18th century. In this type of decoration the cutting tools are beveled, which gives a jewel-like quality to the facets, allowing them to reflect light.

BRITANNIA METAL
An alloy of the 19th and 20th centuries that is generally 93 percent tin, 5 percent antimony, and 2 percent copper. It is very pewterlike and has a silvery look. It was extensively used as a base for electroplating silver, and the initials EPBM, which are sometimes found on the base of objects, stands for "Electro Plated Britannia Metal."

BRITANNIA STANDARD
This is a very pure form of silver consisting of 958 parts pure metal with just 42 parts of base metal such as copper. This standard, which was originally used in England from 1697 to 1720, was established to stop the melting down of coins. The standard was used in America by the Gorham Company for their Martele line, because it was softer than sterling silver and more easily worked by hand.

BRONZE
This is the name given to a wide range of alloys made from copper, zinc, and tin. Arsenic is sometimes found in bronze. It was sometimes added to make the metal harder, but it is often found in the metal as an impurity rather than as a planned addition. In the 20th century, silicon was sometimes added to copper to make a type of bronze. Bronze was used in ancient times for making blades and later for crafting canons, bells, and statuary.

CAM
An eccentric (not circular) wheel that is mounted on a shaft that has the ability to rotate. It is used to produce motion in a mechanism.

CARTOUCHE
An enclosure that holds inscriptions, decorations, initials, names, or heraldic devices. These can be very elaborate, but they can also be as simple as a rectangle or an oval.

CASTING
The process of forming a metal object—particularly silver—by pouring molten metal into a mold. The mold consists of an iron frame (called a "cask"), which holds casting sand that has been impressed with a pattern or design.

CHASING
The process of decorating the surface of a metal object by embossing a design using a punch and a hammer. In this method, the metal is pushed into an impressed decorative pattern, and none of the metal is lost or removed from the surface.

COIN SILVER
This silver standard was widely used in the United States before the Civil War. It refers to silver items that were made by melting down silver coins to obtain the raw material. American coins made from 1792 to 1837 were 89.2 percent pure silver, and those made after 1837 were 90 percent pure silver. Before 1792, American coin silver was made from coins with varying amounts of purity.

DATE-LETTER OR DATE-MARK
A mark of a letter of the alphabet placed on the piece to indicate the year of manufacture. These date letters have been in use in England for more than half a millennium. They do not occur on American silver until the 19th century, and then they are generally symbols rather than letters of the alphabet. Gorham is an exception to this in that they used letters of the alphabet from "A" to "Q" from 1866 to 1884, and then switched to symbols such as bells, roosters, axes, acorns, and anvils. The Steiff Company of Baltimore used letters of the alphabet as well in the 1930s and '40s, but used numbers and symbols otherwise. Reed and Barton and Whiting Manufacturing had dating systems that used symbols rather than alphabet letters.

DIE
A stamp used to impress a design or maker's mark into a metal object.

ELECTROLYSIS
The process of passing an electric current through a conductive liquid

and causing the components of that liquid to be liberated at the two poles (one positive, one negative).

ELECTROPLATE
This process starts with an object that has been made from a base metal such as Britannia or copper. It is then placed in a conducting liquid that has silver or gold in the solution. An electric current is run through the solution, causing ions of the gold or silver to adhere to the surface of the base metal object. This process is called "electrolysis."

EMBOSSING
Decorative process that produces raised designs or lettering on the surface of a metal object.

EPNS
These initials are sometimes found on silver plate and stand for "Electroplated Nickel Silver." Other initials that are found include "EPC," "electroplate on copper"; "EPBM," "electroplated Britannia metal"; and "EPWM," "electroplated white metal."

FLAGON
A tall vessel with handle, spout, and usually a lid. This type of vessel was used to hold wine and in some cases liquor or beer.

FILLET
A narrow strip of flat molding used as a separation between design elements or as an ornamentation to relieve the monotony of long unbroken lines.

FINIAL
The uppermost ornament on the top of an object. It is often shaped like a flame or a ball.

FLATWARE
Utensils used for setting a table such as knives, forks, spoons, and other flat serving pieces such as plates and some platters. This designation does not include such "flat" items as trays and waiters, which are technically considered hollowware.

FORGING
The process of making a metal object by heating a rod or sheet of metal and then shaping it into the desired form by hitting it with a hammer against an anvil or stake. As the shaping process progresses, the metal needs to be reheated from time to time to keep it malleable.

GERMAN SILVER
A silver-colored metal made from nickel, copper, and zinc. It was often used as a base metal for electroplating.

GILDING
The process of applying a small amount of gold to the surface of another metal or substance. Early on, it was often done by combining gold with mercury and painting this mixture onto a metal surface and then heating it to evaporate the mercury. Gilding done in this way was often called "vermeil." This process, however, was outlawed in the 19th century because the mercury was harmful to the workers. Most gilding done since the mid-19th century has been accomplished by electroplating.

GILL
A unit of liquid measure equal to 4 fluid ounces or 1/4 pint in the United States. In Great Britain a gill is 5 fluid ounces or 1/4 pint. In the United States, a gill is 23.656 milliliters; in Britain 28.423 milliliters.

GOLDSMITH
A skilled worker in either gold or silver. The term "silversmith" did not come into wide use until the mid-18th century.

GUILLOCHE
An architectural term that refers to a border formed from two or more bands that are interlaced in such a way as to produce a circular or rounded design that repeats.

HALLMARK
In its most correct usage, this term refers to the marks stamped onto the surface of silver and gold in the Assay

Offices of the English Goldsmiths' Company to certify metal content and identify the location of the Assay Office, the date of manufacture, the goldsmith who made the piece, and in some cases, whether or not the appropriate taxes had been paid. Marks punched into American silver are often referred to as being "hallmarks," but this is technically not correct.

HOLLOWWARE
Hollow vessels such as pitchers, bowls, mugs, teapots, and coffeepots. This term also encompasses flat items used for serving that are not hollow in nature, such as trays and waiters.

JAPANNING
This refers to a coating of varnishlike paint applied to a tinplated form that is then baked in a kiln to produce a black background that resembles Asian lacquer. This coating is good for receiving painted decoration, and it also prevents corrosion of the metal. A type of japanning can also be done to wood.

MASK
The representation of a human or animal head as part of the decoration. These are often fanciful, idealized, or grotesque, and they generally appear in medallions or as terminals at the end of handles.

NICKEL SILVER
This is another name for German silver. When used as a base metal for silver plating, the initials "E. P. N. S." (Electro Plated Nickel Silver) designate that this is the base metal underneath the thin layer of precious metal.

OXIDIZING
The process of darkening certain areas on a piece of silver for decorative effect or to emphasize the design. This is accomplished by using a sulfur compound to tarnish the surface. Great care must be taken by subsequent owners not to remove these areas during the polishing process because it will diminish the decorative effect and devalue the silver. In other words, this is "tarnish" that needs to be left alone.

PARCEL-GILDING
A type of gilding that covers only certain areas of the metal surface. The places that are not to be gilded are covered with a material resistant to the gold.

PATINA
The condition of the surface of an object that, in the case of some metals, is caused by years of polishing, which leaves behind a myriad of tiny scratches. This gives the surface of a piece of silver, for example, a very pleasant, soft lustrous finish. Long, deep scratches are damage and not patina.

PEWTER
A metal alloy that is generally 85 to 96 percent tin with the other metal components being copper, lead, bismuth, or antimony. "Fine pewter," which is designed to be used for eating vessels, is generally 96 percent tin and 4 percent copper with no lead content. "Trifle" pewter was often used to make such things as drinking mugs, and was normally made from 92 percent tin with additions of antimony to make up the balance, although some sources say that as much as 4 percent lead was sometimes used. "Lay" pewter is the lowest quality of the various types of pewter and might be as much as 15 percent lead. This type of pewter tends to be dark and was used to make items that would not be used for food service. Modern pewter is a mixture of tin, copper, antimony, and/or bismuth.

PORRINGER
In American metalware, a porringer is a bowl with one flat, pierced handle perpendicular to the rim of the bowl. In England the "porringer" has two handles and is called a "caudle cup." Examples with two handles and a cover are called an "Ecuelle." In England, the single-handled cup that resembles the American porringer was

used as a "cupping" or bleeding bowl. The porringer was used for a number of purposes on this side of the Atlantic, but the main one was as a bowl for cereal such as porridge, or other foods that might be served to children or those who were bedridden. There are, however, records of these vessels being used for such widely diverse purposes as drinking milk and mixing cosmetics.

PROVENANCE

The record of where an object has been since its origin. This can be very important for works of art and important antiques and can raise monetary values and collector interest exponentially.

REPOUSSÉ

Raised decoration created by hammering from the underneath. Usually, once the hammering from underneath was done, the top surface was chased to add detail and outline. This method of decoration has a long history, but it was introduced to the United States in 1828 by Samuel Kirk, who worked in Baltimore. This is also the name given to one of Kirk's most successful flatware patterns, which is still being made today.

ROCOCO

A decorative style that originated in France during the middle years of the 18th century. The term is derived from the words "rocailles" and "coquilles" or rocks and shells, and refers to decorative motifs that include shells, scrolls (particularly "C" scrolls), floral motifs, and curved lines all arranged asymmetrically. This is one of the most influential styles ever conceived, and it is still being widely used on metalwork in the 21st century.

STERLING SILVER

This is a silver standard that originated in England and is 925 parts pure silver for every 1,000 parts of metal. The other 75 parts per thousand are generally copper. The sterling standard was used in Baltimore from 1800 to 1814, but it was not widely used in the rest of the United States until after the Civil War. The adoption of this standard was urged by Tiffany's and they were instrumental in its adoption. The Stamping Act of 1906 required that all items marked "sterling" be 92.5 percent pure silver.

THUMBPIECE

A raised protrusion above the hinge on a covered vessel such as a tankard. It is used to raise the lid by placing the thumb on the raised portion and pushing down while the rest of the hand grasps the handle.

TIN OR TINPLATE

A type of metal made from thin sheets of iron coated with tin to prevent rust and provide a brighter surface. Tinplating was done by the Romans, but was not commercially viable until the 16th century in Bohemia.

TOLE

Taken from the French word for "sheet metal," "Tole" is properly applied to any decorated or undecorated tinplated ware made in France. Most nonspecialist dictionaries say the Tole is always decorated, but to purist collectors, the term "Tole" includes undecorated examples as well. The term should not be applied to tinware made in countries other than France.

TROY WEIGHT

Derived from the French town Troyes, this term describes a system of weights and measures used primarily in the United States and Great Britain in which one pound equals 12 ounces, one ounce equals 20 pennyweights (abbreviated "dwt."), and one pennyweight equals 24 grains or one-twentieth of an ounce. Expressed another way, one pound avoirdupois (from the French for "good of weight," the system used every day to measure such things as nonprecious metals, fruit, and vegetables, and such) equals 14.58 Troy ounces, and one pound Troy equals 13.165 ounces avoirdupois.

VERMEIL
This is a name given to gilded metal, usually silver, but it can be applied to gilded bronze or copper as well. It is the result of a gold-plating process that originated in Roman times and was revived in France in the 18th century. The process involved the use of an amalgam of mercury, pumice, and alum plus gold leaf. It was outlawed in the 19th century because of the use of poisonous mercury, and electroplating began to be used to apply the thin layer of gold.

WALDO
This gold-colored metal alloy is made by the Holmes and Edwards Silver Company of Bridgeport, Connecticut, which marked these wares with "Waldo HE." The principal ingredient in this metal is aluminum, and it was first made in 1894. "Waldo" metal is also called "gold aluminum."

WHITE METAL
An alloy of metals such as tin, copper, lead, antimony, and bismuth. Sometimes called "pot metal," it is an inexpensive metal used for making everything from pots and pans to statuary.

WHITESMITH
A highly skilled worker of tin, who made pieces by hammering rather than by casting. A whitesmith is also a highly skilled worker of iron, an armorer.

Bibliography and Additional Reading

Bertoia, Jeanne. *Doorstops, Identification and Values.* Paducah, KY: Collector Books, 1985.

Bishop, Robert, and Patricia Coblentz. *A Gallery of American Weathervanes and Whirligig.* New York: E. P. Dutton and Company, 1981.

Carpenter, Charles H. *Gorham Silver 1831–1981.* New York: Dodd, Mead & Company, 1982.

Coffin, Margaret. *The History and Folklore of American Country Tinware 1700–1900.* Camden, NJ: Thomas Nelson & Sons, 1968.

Duer, Don. *A Penny Saved: Still and Mechanical Banks.* Altglen, PA: Schiffer Publishing Ltd., 1993.

Kaye, Myrna. *Yankee Weathervanes.* New York: E. P. Dutton and Company, 1975.

Kovel, Ralph M., and Terry H. *A Dictionary of American Silver, Pewter, and Silver Plate.* New York: Crown Publishers, Inc., 1961.

Laughlin, Ledlie Irwin. *Pewter in America: Its Makers and Their Marks.* New York: American Legacy Press, 1981.

Rainwater, Dorothy T. *Encyclopedia of American Silver Manufacturers.* Altglen, PA: Schiffer Publishing Ltd., 1986.

Rainwater, Dorothy T., and H. Ivan. *American Silverplate.* Nashville, TN: Thomas Nelson Inc. and Hanover, PA: Everybodys Press, 1968.

Schiffer, Peter, Nancy, and Herbert. *The Brass Book: American, English, and European Fifteenth Century through 1850.* Exton, PA: Schiffer Publishing, Ltd., 1978.

Venable, Charles L. *Silver in America 1840–1940: A Century of Splendor.* Dallas: Dallas Museum of Art, and New York: Harry B. Abrams, 1994.

Photo Credits

Item #1 "Highlander" Fireback
Item courtesy of Northeast Auctions, Portsmouth, New Hampshire

Item #2 "Judith" Fireback
Item courtesy of Northeast Auctions, Portsmouth, New Hampshire

Item #3 Wafer Iron
Item courtesy of the collection of Jeffery Cupp

Item #4 Iron and Brass Candlestand
Item courtesy of Northeast Auctions, Portsmouth, New Hampshire

Item #5 Griswold Skillet
Item courtesy of the collection of Roger Welsh
Photograph by Richard H. Crane

Related Item Griswold Baking Dish
Item courtesy of the collection of Elaine Tomber Tindell
Photograph by Richard H. Crane

Item #6 Golfer Doorstop
Item courtesy of Skinner, Inc., Boston and Bolton, Massachusetts

Item #7 House Doorstop
Item courtesy of Bertoia Auction Gallery, Vineland, New Jersey

Item #8 Squirrel Mill Weight
Item courtesy of Northeast Auctions, Portsmouth, New Hampshire

Related Item Bull Mill Weight
Item courtesy of Northeast Auctions, Portsmouth, New Hampshire

Related Item Rooster Mill Weight
Item courtesy of Northeast Auctions, Portsmouth, New Hampshire

Item #9 "Possum and Taters" Still Bank
Item courtesy of Bertoia Auction Gallery, Vineland, New Jersey

Related Item "Indian Family" Still Bank
Item courtesy of Bertoia Auction Gallery, Vineland, New Jersey

Item #10 Bank Building Mechanical Bank
Item courtesy of Skinner, Inc., Boston and Bolton, Massachusetts

Item #11 "Tammany" Mechanical Bank
Item courtesy of Bertoia Auction Gallery, Vineland, New Jersey

Item #12 "Uncle Sam" Mechanical Bank
Item courtesy of Bertoia Auction Gallery, Vineland, New Jersey

Item #13 "Lighthouse" Semi-Mechanical Bank
Item courtesy of Skinner, Inc., Boston and Bolton, Massachusetts.

Item #14 "Jonah and the Whale" Pull Toy
Item courtesy of Skinner, Inc., Boston and Bolton, Massachusetts

Item #15 Horse-Drawn Sleigh Toy
Item courtesy of Bertoia Auction Gallery, Vineland, New Jersey

Item #16 *Andy Gump* Car
Item courtesy of Bertoia Auction Gallery, Vineland, New Jersey

Item #17 Vindex Truck
Item courtesy of Bertoia Auction Gallery, Vineland, New Jersey

Item #18 Buddy-L Truck
Item courtesy of Skinner, Inc., Boston and Bolton, Massachusetts

Item #19 Painted Document Box
Item courtesy of Skinner, Inc., Boston and Bolton, Massachusetts

Item #20 Lantern
Item courtesy of Northeast Auctions, Portsmouth, New Hampshire

Related Item Painted Coffeepot
Item courtesy of Skinner, Inc., Boston and Bolton, Massachusetts

Item #21 Candle Sconces
Item courtesy of Northeast Auctions, Portsmouth, New Hampshire

Item #22 Quatrefoil Candle Sconces
Item courtesy of Northeast Auctions, Portsmouth, New Hampshire

Item #23 Chandelier
Item courtesy of Northeast Auctions, Portsmouth, New Hampshire

Item #24 Drugstore Sign
Item courtesy of Skinner, Inc., Boston and Bolton, Massachusetts

Item #25 "Tintype" Photograph
Item courtesy of the collection of Dr. Bob Paddleford
Photograph by Richard H. Crane

Item #26 Popeye with Punching Bag
Item courtesy of Bertoia Auction Gallery, Vineland, New Jersey

Related Item Popeye with Overhead Punching Bag
Item courtesy of Bertoia Auction Gallery, Vineland, New Jersey

Item #27 Mickey and Minnie Mouse Washing Machine
Item courtesy of Bertoia Auction Gallery, Vineland, New Jersey

Item #28 Thomas D. and Sherman Boardman Flagon
Item courtesy of Skinner, Inc., Boston and Bolton, Massachusetts

Item #29 Thomas Danforth III Dish
Item courtesy of Skinner, Inc., Boston and Bolton, Massachusetts

Item #30 Samuel Hamlin Quart Mug
Item courtesy of Skinner, Inc., Boston and Bolton, Massachusetts

Item #31 Hasselberg Group Plate
Item courtesy of the collection of Jeff Cupp

Item #32 George Washington Inaugural Button
Item courtesy of Skinner, Inc. Boston and Bolton, Massachusetts

Item #33 Gorham Mixed Metals Bowl
Item courtesy of Skinner, Inc., Boston and Bolton, Massachusetts

Related Item Gorham Mixed Metals Lamp Base
Item courtesy of Skinner, Inc., Boston and Bolton, Massachusetts

Item #34 Tiffany Mixed Metals Bowl
Item courtesy of Skinner, Inc., Boston and Bolton, Massachusetts

Item #35 Saint Gaudens Bust
Item courtesy of Skinner, Inc., Boston and Bolton, Massachusetts

Item #36 Bradley and Hubbard Bookend
Item courtesy of Bertoia Auction Gallery, Vineland, New Jersey

Item #37 "Goddess of Liberty" Weathervane
Item courtesy of Northeast Auctions, Portsmouth, New Hampshire

Item #38 A. L. Jewel "Centaur" Weathervane
Item courtesy of Skinner, Inc., Boston and Bolton, Massachusetts

Item #39 Gamecock Weathervane
Item courtesy of Skinner, Inc., Boston and Bolton, Massachusetts

Item #40 Daguerreotype of Millard Fillmore
Item courtesy of Skinner, Inc., Boston and Bolton, Massachusetts

Related Item Daguerreotype of an Unknown Subject
Item courtesy of the collection of Richard H. Crane
Photograph by Richard H. Crane

Item #41 Philadelphia Andirons
Item courtesy of Skinner, Inc., Boston and Bolton, Massachusetts

Item #42 R. Wittingham Andirons
Item courtesy of Northeast Auctions, Portsmouth, New Hampshire

Item #43 Skimmer
Item courtesy of Northeast Auctions, Portsmouth, New Hampshire

Item #44 Candlesticks
Item courtesy of the collection of Jeff Cupp

Item #45 Samuel Edwards Butter Plate
Item courtesy of Skinner, Inc., Boston and Bolton, Massachusetts

Item #46 Collection of 6 Spoons
Items courtesy of the collection of Jeff Cupp
Photograph by Richard H. Crane

Item #47 Paul Revere Tablespoon
Item courtesy of Northeast Auctions, Portsmouth, New Hampshire

Item #48 Kirk Flatware, "Repousse"
Item courtesy of the collection of Burton and Helaine Fendelman
Photograph by Richard H. Crane

Related Item Kirk Tea Set, "Repousse"
Item courtesy of Replacements, Ltd., Greensboro, North Carolina

Item #49 Reed and Barton Fish Slice, "Trajan"
Item courtesy of the collection of Richard H. Crane
Photograph by Richard H. Crane

Item #50 Reed and Barton Flatware, "Francis I"
Item courtesy of Replacements, Ltd., Greensboro, North Carolina

Item #51 Dominick and Haff Flatware, "Labors of Cupid"
Item courtesy of Replacements, Ltd., Greensboro, North Carolina

Item #52 Tiffany Pitcher, "Wave Edge"
Item courtesy of Replacements, Ltd., Greensboro, North Carolina

Related Item Tiffany Flatware, "Wave Edge"
Item courtesy of Replacements, Ltd., Greensboro, North Carolina

Item #53 Tiffany Tilt Cradle Hot-Water Kettle, "Chrysanthemum"
Item courtesy of Replacements, Ltd., Greensboro, North Carolina

Related Item Tiffany Flatware, "Chrysanthemum"

Item #54 Tiffany Demitasse Coffee Set, "English King"
Item courtesy of Replacements, Ltd., Greensboro, North Carolina

Item #55 Gebelein Flatware
Item courtesy of Skinner, Inc., Boston and Bolton, Massachusetts

Item #56 Gorham Candelabra, "Buttercup"
Item courtesy of Replacements, Ltd., Greensboro, North Carolina

Related Item Gorham Flatware, "Buttercup"
Item courtesy of Replacements, Ltd., Greensboro, North Carolina

Item #57 Simon, Bro. and Company Match Safe
Item courtesy of the collection of Richard H. Crane
Photograph by Richard H. Crane

Item #58 Pairpoint Basket
Item courtesy of the collection of Betsey B. Creekmore
Photograph by Richard H. Crane

Item #59 Barbour Vase
Item courtesy of the collection of Dr. and Mrs. Chalmer Chastain
Photograph by Richard H. Crane

Item #60 Middletown Plate Company Jam Jar
Item courtesy of the collection of Dr. and Mrs. Chalmer Chastain
Photograph by Richard H. Crane

Item #61 Derby Silver Company Creamer
Item courtesy of the collection of Dr. and Mrs. Chalmer Chastain
Photograph by Richard H. Crane

Item #62 Reed and Barton Tea Set
Item courtesy of the collection of Dr. and Mrs. Chalmer Chastain
Photograph by Richard H. Crane

Index